9.3, 2022,
Mom

Prayers for Black Women

God Still heals

Janie McGee
Editor Ramon McGee

Much Love from

Ramon and Janie McGee
and the Grandchildren &
Great Grandchildren

Special Thanks

Special thanks to God, Jesus, and the Holy Spirit. To my husband, co-author and best friend - Ramon McGee. To our son Jamile McGee our daughter Jasmine McGee - Ventura and John Ventura, and Gabriel McGee our grandson, London Stuart, our granddaughter, Robert Dillard and Louise Dillard who are in heaven with God, All my brothers and sisters: Pinky, Jay, Wanda, Charles, Billy, Tony, and Dee. Also to all of my sisters-in-law, cousins, nephews, nieces, aunts, and uncles in the Dillard family. Ann McGee, Ramona McGee, Simone McGee, Special thanks to my uncle Nate Fitzgerald who has gone on to heaven, George Horton Jr. The Horton Family, Andrea Stewart, Santwan Barksdale, Andre and Sherri Ballard, and our Elder Lavelle Roe who is gone to be with the Lord.

"The past holds the key to the tidal wave of hope
That vision births in the future"

double latte books
Ramon and Janie McGee

Prayers for Black Women
God Still Heals...

Copyright © 2018 by Janie McGee

The clip art used in this book is Microsoft Office software.
All rights reserved by Janie McGee. Cover Art royal Free and designed by Janie McGee

Visit Our Website www.doublelattebooks.net
And www.seejanedream.com

Contents

Prayer and Salvation

Coffee with God! This book is designed to encourage us as Black people to pray, pray effectively and spend time with God. It begins with you praying and getting right with God. God can and will use you in prayer for others. This book is for you to grow in prayer and grow in Christ. The prayers in this book are not formulas to follow. They are prayers to inspire you to pray with power for yourself and others in your walk with God. Pray always in the Holy Spirit no matter what you do. This book is for those who know Christ. If you do not have a relationship with him then take the first step and pray asking Jesus to come into your heart and for the Holy Spirit to fill your heart. You need power in these last days to know God. The power begins when you begin to grow in Christ.

There are many people in the body of Christ who are babies and have never grown past just attending church. Jesus is power! He is awesome! He died for you to know him! He answers prayer! He will make a way out of no way if you trust him Try Jesus! Take a few minutes and pray if you don't know him. And if you are backslidden in any way then ask him to restore you to a place in him. It doesn't take just going to church and walking down to the altar to get things right, but just a prayer from the heart to have him refresh and jump start your walk with him all over again. Jesus loves you and is waiting! Make today a new day for him!

" For God so loved the world that he gave His only begotten Son, that whosoever believeth in him should not perish, but have everlasting life. "
John 3:16 KJV

"Receive ye the Holy Ghost "
John 20:22 KJV

"That if you would confess with thy mouth the Lord Jesus and shall believe in your heart that God hath raised him from the dead, you shall be saved. " Romans 10:9 KJV

Sinner's Prayer

Heavenly Father, I come to you in prayer asking forgiveness for my sins. I repent of all my sins. I believe that Jesus died for my sins and was resurrected, sitting on the right hand of the Father. Through Jesus, I believe I have eternal life. I believe that His death and resurrection provided for my forgiveness. I trust in Jesus and Jesus alone as my personal Lord and Savior. Thank you, Lord, for saving me and forgiving me! I ask you right now to come into my heart and I give you my life. I accept Jesus as my personal savior. I confess with my mouth that I am born again. Fill me with your Holy Spirit and cleanse me, Lord.

Make me new in you. I receive your Holy Spirit and can begin a new life now in you Jesus. Help and guide me daily to read your word and to walk with you, God. In Jesus' name Amen.

Backslider?

You may be someone who has already accepted Jesus Christ as your Lord and Savior. Maybe you accepted Him years ago but have fallen out of fellowship with Him, or lived so long in sin that your relationship with Jesus is not right, and you know it. There's good news for you. A restored relationship with Jesus is just a prayer away.

"If we confess our sins, he is faithful and just to forgive us our sins and to cleanse us from all righteousness." 1 John 1:9 KJV

Backslider's Prayer

Lord Jesus, I confess that my heart and life have not been responsive, as I need to be in following you. I am tired of backsliding in my life, my heart, and my soul and into sin. Lord, please cleanse me from my sins of thought and deeds. Please allow your cleansing blood to flow through my hardened, broken heart. Please give me new life in my heart and revive it according to your righteousness. Please restore me to you Jesus in the fullness of your word. Restore to me my sensitivity to you and help me to see sin as you see it. Refresh me with your Holy Spirit and fill me to overflowing with your love. Give me the power to walk with you and follow you every day. Lead me Holy Spirit, re-fill me, and teach me to pray!

11

Jesus, please give me the strength and commitment to move forward confidently and walk with you in obedience daily. I offer my entire being, body, soul, and spirit, to do your will, to worship you, and walk with you from this point on. Thank you for helping me. I pray this in the name of Jesus Christ. Amen."

Restores Fellowship to Hear from God Prayer

Father God, though I once accepted Jesus Christ as my Lord and Savior, I have not been spending time with Jesus. I have not been talking to him, spending time in His word, or praying like I know I should. Father, you said if I would confess my sins, you are faithful and just to forgive me of all of my sins. I confess my sins of walking away from Jesus, and not spending time with Him like I should. Please forgive me for all of my sins Father God in the name of Jesus Christ. Restore my relationship and fellowship with You Father God, and with Your Son Jesus Christ. Help me to hear you clearly, daily Lord. Open up my ears to hear and my heart to receive! Fill me anew and afresh with your mighty Holy Spirit, the Comforter who leads and guides me into all the truth in Jesus' name. Thank You, Father God for restoring my relationship with Jesus Christ in the name of Jesus Christ.

My sheep hear my voice, and I know them and they follow me: And I give unto them eternal life: and they shall never perish, neither shall any man pluck them out of my hand. "John 10:27-28

12

Note...

The last 6 chapters of this are teachings on healing and more. You can go to that section now or go straight to the prayers the first section of this book.

Note to you!

We are not medical doctors. We are Prayer warriors. We are not in the medical field. We are called to encourage prayer for those in the body of Christ. Let the doctors watch over you, as you anticipated God's healing you. Use wisdom in making sure you take medication, follow your doctor order, and do those things medically you need to do. We do not prescribe stopping the use of medicines or any routines your doctor have given you for your personal health issues. The purpose of this book is spiritual, not medical to pray through and believe God for miracles in your health spirit, soul, and body. Use wisdom and do what you are supposed to do as you see God manifest your miracle. Get the mind of God over ever decision you make. Be prayerful! Pray changes thing and it is power. We believe that God can manifest healing and have your doctor confirm it. Until then, stay on course with your proscribes routines and medicines. And when God does heal . Give him the praise; give him the glory for your manifested miracle. We are not liable or responsible for the outcome that you or your doctors do not find favorable. We highly recommend following your doctor's prescribed orders. As prayer warrior, we believe for your healing! Get the Mind of God over decision! The goal is to put the book down and just pray as you are led by the Holy Ghost!!

My prayer for you

I pray God builds your faith, heals you, your family, friends, and loved ones. May God show forth his power on your behalf. May this book be anointed with healing and miracles to give God all the glory for what you are facing spirit, soul, and body. Holy Spirit please fall on them, refresh them, touch them and lead the reader of this books to feel you move in them. Teach them to prayer and change their lives and others by your power in Jesus name. Not our will lord, but your will be done in Jesus name! Fill each page with power in Jesus name. Have your way lord! Speak to and through your people. Be glorified in their healing! In Jesus name, I Pray!

Prayers for the Soul & Mind
Chapter 1
"You keep him in perfect peace whose mind is stayed on you because he trusts in you." Isaiah 26:2

"Let us draw near with a sincere heart in full assurance of faith, having our hearts sprinkled clean from an evil conscience and our bodies washed with pure water." Hebrews 10:22

"You will keep in perfect peace all who trust in you, all whose thoughts are fixed on you!" Isaiah 23:6

Peace of Mind

Father in Heaven, I thank you for your faithfulness to me. Recently I have had a hard time living life without stress, anxiety, and fear. I need you to restore my mind to perfect peace. Jesus, you said you have given us a peace that the world can not take away. I need that peace to get through the storms I am facing. I need you, Lord, to restore and strengthen me with peace of mind. Allow your word to renew my mind to have the mind of Christ. Take away every thought that is not of you. As it says in your word, in your name I pull down every stronghold over my mind and cast down every wicked imagination that tries to overtake me. I bind in Jesus name every demon of stress, worry, fear, anxiety, and torment in my life. I cast you to the desert and dry places in Jesus Name! I break every curse on my mind 40 generations back. I break every wicked prayer and schemes prayed against me from my enemies hindering my peace. I loose, according to your word, that I am whole spirit, soul, and body in Jesus name. You are Jehovah Shalom, the God of peace. I receive your peace right now in Jesus name. I lay all my burdens before you and let them go! I will do as you say and instruct .I pray for wisdom. I will be led by your Holy Spirit daily in all things. Holy Spirit guide me and show me the Father's will. I receive your peace now in my mind. Peace be still in Jesus name.

"For God is not a God of confusion, but of peace."

Confusion

Jehovah Mekoddishkem, the Lord who sanctifies, you have set us apart to be your instruments in the earth. I thank you, God helping me. Lord, there is so much confusion in my life and mind on what your will is. Whatever I have been exposed to that has caused so much confusion in my life I need you to rescue my mind and thoughts. Touch me with your mighty power and clear away all the confusion I have been faced with in my mind lately. Give me a clear path of thoughts to know what your will is. I bind all the demonic voices, whispers, and intimidating attacks from other people's opinions. Lead me to your will. Help me to receive and hear from you. Give me peace and understanding with clarity now, than ever before. Every attack on my thoughts to confuse me, I bind in Jesus name. I rebuke the spirit of confusion over my mind. I break every soul tie with people, things objects, places or events that has caused me to become unclear in my thoughts and actions. I cast them away. I thank you for restoring me now to a state of sanity and clarity in the name of Jesus. Help me to rest my mind, thoughts and meditate on your word day and night. Thank you for clear directions and the ability to make decisions that are in line with your will and your word. You said in your word to get wisdom with understanding. I pray for clear understanding and the strength to do you will on the things I am facing today. Thank you, Jesus, for my deliverance from the spirit of confusion right now! In Jesus name.

"Draw near to my soul, redeem me; ransom me because of my enemies! You know my reproach, and my shame and my dishonor; my foes are all known to you. Reproaches have broken my heart so that I am in despair." Psalm 69:17-18

Wounded/Fragmented Soul

God that comforts the soul, I cry out to you to heal my wounded soul. There is no one greater than you. You are my creator. You created me. You know my comings and goings. You know my hurts and my disappointments. I belong to you Lord. My soul is wounded from all the pain and grief in living life. Heal me, Lord. Give me the strength to forgive others and myself that have hurt me. The pain is so deep I can't get to it, but I know you are able to touch the deepest part of me. I surrender my heart and soul to you to begin the healing in me today. Help me father, to not dwell on the past. Revive in me a vision for my life. Heal my fragmented soul. Give me a new vision for my talents, career, and purpose in you. I open my heart and my wounded soul to you to speak peace and healing over me. I cannot make it without you Lord! Do a deep work in me that repairs the broken bridges in my soul, release me from my fears, take away the tenderness I feel when the wounds are reopened by people, and be glorified in my life through this healings. I do not want to hurt anymore. Therefore, I receive your comfort and healing. Holy Spirit guide me daily to walk out a new perspective and healing in my life as seen by heaven. Jesus, you took all my sins and pains to the cross and because of that, I know I have been set free. In Jesus name amen! I am healed!

"Therefore do not be anxious about tomorrow, for tomorrow will be anxious for itself. Sufficient for the day is its own trouble." Mathew 6:33

Stress Anxiety

Alpha and Omega, all things are in your hands! You rule the stars and the universe! You are Lord over all. I need you holy one of Isreal to take away my anxiety and stress. It is too much for me to bare. I am overwhelmed by the weight of this world. I need deliverance. My finances, family, jobs, friends, and personal plans are too much for me to bear. I give them all to you right now! As I come before you I lay down my burdens at your throne. I don't want to pick them back up again. I leave them here. Every weight, every burden, every fear, every concern, every problem, every hurt, every trial, every distraction, all my anxiety, and my stress, I lay down now before you! Come, now and pour out your peace over my mind, my soul, my heart, my strength, my life! I can't carry it. I won't carry! I give it to you. Every weight of this world I lay it down! I just want to rest and lay at your feet, dear lord. I just need this time with you to get refreshed and feel your love. Pour out your love and power over me now. I weep and cry out to you, lord. I need you now! I lay it all down. Come Holy Spirit and wash over me with you fresh water. Let the anointing flow over me and revive my mind, my soul and spirit. I give you praise Lord and thank you for taking away my burdens. Father, when I get up I leave them here. I will be led by you from here on out. I am restored and refreshed in Jesus name! Praise your name. God of peace. In Jesus name! Amen! Restored!

"In peace will I both lay me down and sleep: for thou, LORD, alone makest me dwell in safety." Psalm 4:8

Tormenting Dreams & Nightmare

Adonia, I call upon you to help me sleep peacefully at night. My sleep is disturbed nightly. I need your power and peace to tonight. I give my rest to you in Jesus name. If there is anything physically causing my sleeplessness, touch me and heal my body. I believe Lord for you to bring the right chemical balance to my body to rest at nightly in you. If there, anything in my soul/mind keeping me from sleeping heal me now. Remove all worries, anxiety, and fears. Take away insomnia, now in Jesus name. I give my burdens to you. I lay them at your feet. If there is anything demonic, that is tormenting me I rebuke it, in Jesus name. I bind it in the name of Jesus. I ask you, Lord, to put the hedge back up of my angels to keep me at night. Any demonic spirits in my dreams or causing nightmare I bind them in the Jesus name I cast them to the desert/dry place. I rebuke every witchcraft prayer against me. I bind sleep paralysis! I call upon you Lord to remove any entities and demonic forces that are in my home. I bless my bedroom, my bed, my home, and the all the objects in my house in your name Jesus. I loose the power of God in the name of Jesus in my home to be a place of peace and safety in Jesus name! I receive a blessed night of sleep from here on out. I will greet you in the morning lords with praise and peace as my sleep has been restored back to peace in Jesus name!

"For it was not an enemy that reproached me; then I could have borne it: neither was it he that hated me that did magnify himself against me; then I would have hid myself from him: But it was thou, a man mine equal, my companion, and my familiar friend· We took sweet counsel together, we walked in the house of God with the throng." Psalm 55:12-13

Social Media

Captain of my salvation, my friend Jesus! Deliver me from social media addiction. Deliver me from Dopamine that causes me to feed on being accepted, liked, and having a positive response on social media platforms. Lord is taking over my life and taking up to much time I could spend with you. Gird up my self-esteem to have Christ-esteem in you. Jesus, you are my friend. You are all I need and more. I need your help not too look to social media or people to have a sense of who I am in you. If you lead me to post anything that would be a blessing, I will. If I am, posting anything to get the glory from you and taking it for myself stop me, lord. Make me whole spirit, soul, and body. Help me to be sincere and real in how I present my walk with you. Do not let me get involved in any social media drama, bad relationships, feuds, adultery, or anything immoral that is not of you. If I need to deactivate any accounts, give me the strength to walk away. If I m being influenced by anything evil deliver me, that I do participate or become a part of the enemy's plans for social media. Set me free from pride and self-exaltation. Give me a sense of self-come from walking with you and not the praise of men. In Jesus name, I pray! Amen!

"For this reason I remind you to fan into flame the gift of God, which is in you through the laying on of my hands, for God gave us a spirit not of fear but of power and love and self-control." 2 timothy1:6-7

Fear

 Almighty Father, I seek your face in prayer today for deliverance from fear. I come to you Lord of all, my refuge, and shelter in a time of need. I have walked in fear for a long time. I need you to deliverer me from being so fearful so I can walk boldly in representing you. I can't of nothing without you. I need your grace and mercy to touch my life with boldness. I am afraid of so many things Lord. Take away the fears and close the entranceway that fear have come into my life. Shut the doors to anything in my imagination and stronghold that have resided in my soul, spirit, and mind. I surrender all my fears to you Lord. Take them away in Jesus name. Deliver me from the torment that fear has caused in my life. Deliver me from the limitations it has placed in my life. Set me free now Jesus by your power. Holy Spirit I surrender and submit myself to you, Lord, I resist the devil and his demons that they must flee! Holy Spirit come now and fall on me with refreshing power. Give me peace and boldness that come from walking with Jesus Christ. I rebuke fear! I bind it in Jesus name! I command it to leave my home and my life forever in Jesus name! Renew my mind and thoughts to see life as Christ Jesus reveals his will in my life. I receive deliverance now from fear. Thanks, Lord, for a new start in walking in boldness, deliverance from fear, and peace in you! The spirit of fear no longer consumes me! In Jesus name, amen!

" If I say, 'I will forget my complaint, I will put off my sad face, and be of good cheer" Job 9:27

Depression & Loneliness

Rock of my salvation, I cry out to you for help with depression. Every day I wake up, I want the day to better than it was before. However, I wake up depressed and sad. I am overwhelmed with life. Take away the sadness and loneliness I feel inside. This depression is taking over my life. Help me! Heal me Lord of any chemical imbalances in my body that are causing me to be depressed, mood swings, and unstable emotions. I look to you to give me joy everlasting in place of the overwhelming sadness. Touch me with your powerful love. Heal my heart, mind, body, memories, and soul. I need you lord inside of me to give me joy. I lay down every burden, weight, issues, money problem, family matters, health issue, and work conflicts before you. I can't carry them anymore. I need you! I cry out to you! I lift is all up to you for miracles, answers, hope, and understanding of the things I am facing. I look to you. Take away the deep loneliness that I feel inside. Wipe away my tears. I feel like I am facing all this by myself. Show your love. Fill my life with power and Spirit! Surround me with true believers, family, and friends that will love and support me. I bind every generational curse that is causing me to inherit depression and other medical issues 40 generations back. Let the joy of the Lord be my strength daily. I receive your hope, deliverance, strength, and a new outlook on my life! Give me a hunger for you! I am healed! Put a new song in my heart! The joy of the Lord is my strength! I have new hope! New Smile! I can see my life now in a new light. I am delivered! My burdens are lifting! Thanks, you Jesus for restoring my joy. I praise you, Lord! My soul is restored! I am made whole! Glory to your holy name! In Jesus name! Amen!

"You keep him in perfect peac3 whose mind is stayed on you, because he trusts in you." Isaiah 26:2

Dementia & Alzheimer

The Creator of Heaven and Earth, great is thy mercy toward us! As we age on this earth, we are faced with many struggles. Nevertheless, there is nothing too hard for you. My mind is in battles to hold fast thoughts, memories, time, and sometimes words. Touch me with your mercy and grace. I believe you can heal me. I have hope in you. I am holding on lord to you. My physical body is trying to slip away and my mind wants to go with it. Every daily task has been very hard. I need you now more than ever, father. I ask in your mercy and grace that you give me the ability to think clearly, hold my thoughts, hold on to memories, and live daily with a clear understanding of the world around me. Deliver me from the chaos and confusion that seem to take over my mind. I feel like I have no control over what is going in me, but you do lord. Jesus, you took every infirmity I face to the cross. You were born, lived, died, and rose again for all things I have to face. You have been there for me. I call upon you, to heal my mind and straighten out the medical, emotions, and the troublesome path I am on right now in my mind. Heal me of Dementia. Heal me Lord of early stages Alzheimer. Heal me of all Alzheimer. I believe with all my heart, you are able and willing. I submit my mind to you that you heal and restore my mind, as I grow older to be strong, consistent, and accurate daily. Lord, you are all I have. I look to you. I thank you for the doctors you have provided. I thank you for the family has shown me patience. I look to you to heal my mind and help me to remember the past and walk out life today with clear thoughts. I believe my memories and my mind have been made whole are restore to you. Not my will Lord, but your will be done. I praise and you and thank you for another that I can have clarity in my mind. Give my family the strength they need to walk thoughts this trial. Each day from here out, I look for a miracle in my mind and health that I can glory you. In Jesus name, I pray Amen!

"For if the blood of goats and bulls, and the sprinkling of defiled persons with the ashes of a heifer, sanctify for the purification of the flesh, 14 how much more will the blood of Christ, who through the eternal Spirit offered himself without blemish to God, purify our conscience from dead works to serve the living God."   Hebrew 9:13-14

Drugs, Cigarettes & Alcohol Addictions

King of Kings and Lord of Lords, there is nothing too hard for you. I seek your face for freedom from addictions. My life has been consumed and destroyed by my addictions. I need your divine intervention. First, I rededicate my life back to you. I surrender my life to you, Jesus. I believe you died upon the cross and rose again. I repent of all my sins. I have turned to substances to heal my inner pain, but now I turn to you. I need your power and deliverance to set me free. Holy Spirit gives me power now to set free. Fill me now! I surrender and submit myself to you, Lord, I resist the demons and devil that they must free. I bind all demons of bondage and addictions in my life. I cast them to the desert and dry place. I bind the appetite in my soul and, body and mind for substances. Heal my mind and brain from the desire to use substances. I bind every generational curse that has caused me to have an addiction. I bind every demon that I inherited from the use of drugs and alcohol in my life. I cast them far from me. I loose the healing power of God over my life to restore all the damage that has been done in my body from the substance. I Loose sobriety over my life. I seek you Holy Father to pour out your presence in my life. Remove every friend or relationship I have with those involved with addiction. Shut the door and covenants I have made with people and demonic spirit to participate I the addictions. Wash me now and make me holy.

Cleanse my whole being from the residue of the substance abuse. Take away any desire I have to return to the addiction in your name Jesus I have been set free. Restore my job; talents, purpose, and livelihood that have been hindering the addiction. Restore my relationship with my family and friends. Help them to forgive me for my downfall. Restore all my finance that has been affected by addiction. Provide finance for any medical expenses and rehab I have accrued during this trial. Jesus, my savior walks me toward a new vision and way of life without the addictions and bondage. Show me how to achieve and live the purpose you have for me daily. Open doors for any future rehab. Deliver me form any legal issues. I pray I find favor with the courts. I am victorious in you Lord. I receive 100% deliverance right now. I praise you for the breakthrough. Every day walk me toward a stable new path. I receive permanent deliverance from the spirit of bondage and addiction that was in my life. I am cover by the blood of Jesus. I am set free. Create in me an appetite for your word. Guide me to fellowship with you daily. Lord, replace the addiction with a desire for you. No weapon formed against me will prosper. Let the Holy Spirit guide me and strengthen me all the day of my life. I glorify your name Lord for my deliverance. Teach me to stand on this deliverance and to war in the spirit to stay set free. I give you name the praise and glory In Jesus name. Amen!

"Blessed are those who mourn, for they shall be comforted." Mathew 5:3

PTSD/ Tormenting Spirits

Abba, Father I need your help with PTSD and tormenting spirit. I thank you, Lord, for surviving the worst tragedy imagined in my life. I did not know how I would survive it, but you brought me through. Things may not be the same in my life, but I am grateful for a second chance. I need your comfort! Lord my thoughts, mind, emotions, life, and daily existence it still affected by those events. I need your divine intervention in my life. Every day has been hard. I need help managing the emotions and mental repercussion from the event I lived through. I am tormented by the events with nightmares, fears, and limitation on my life. I feel like I am at war inside my mind. It has been hard to cope and live normal. I believe that because you let me survive those events you have a plan. You are also able to deliver me from the PTSD and tormenting thoughts from the events that almost destroyed my life. Set me free from every stronghold that has tried to settle into my life. I bind suicide spirits. I will live and not die! I bind every demon and tormenting spirit that has had an entranceway through the events that happen. I cast them far from me. Touch my heart, mind, and soul to be a threefold cord not broken by the tragedy. Make me whole; deliver me from the nightmares, thoughts, emotion, internal war, and fears. Set me free from the uncontrollable reaction I have, due to the event that happen. Make me whole in Jesus name. The blood of Jesus forever delivers me delivered today from PTSD and tormenting spirit. I receive your peace Jesus in my life to keep me. In Jesus name! I walk toward my future in you and leave the past behind. Help Jesus!

"Blessed be the God and Father of our Lord Jesus Christ, the Father of mercies and God of all comfort, who comforts us in all our affliction, so that we may be able to comfort those who are in any affliction, with the comfort with which we ourselves are comforted by God. For as we share abundantly in Christ's sufferings, so through Christ we share abundantly in comfort too." 2 Corinthians 1: 3-5

Divorce & Break Up

God of Love, the mender of broken hearts, I need you to give me the strength to get through this separation from someone I once loved. I never imagine I would have to say goodbye to them, but I need help walking away. Unless it is in your will to restore the relationship, I walk away Lord. Guide my heart on your will. The pain is very hard to bear. I give you full permission to place this in your perfect will. I am hurting inside Lord. My heart is ripped out. Come now and put the pieces back together. Restore my life from the devastating circumstances that this relationship has caused. Help me to still walk in love. I cry out for forgiveness to you for anything I have done. I also ask you to help me forgive them for the hurt and pain they have caused. I pray for closure that I can walk away with the peace Break the soul ties I have with them. I have done my best. I pray for my Ex that you heal that and give them the future you have prepared. Father, heal me over time. Prepare me for the next relationship that you have. Build me up and give me the tools I need to have a stronger better God center relationship in the future. I will wait for you. I pray you help me to use the time of waiting and healing to grow closer to you God. I will love again! I thank you, Jesus, for being a healer of my heart. In Jesus name! Amen!

"That the generation to come might know that the children should be born; should arise and declare to their children: That they might set their hope in God, and not forget the works of God, but keep his commandments: And might not be as their fathers, a stubborn and rebellious generation; a generation set not their heart aright, and whose spirit was not steadfast with God."
Psalm 76:6-8

Children Stress

Lord of all Mankind, I seek your face for my children. I am stressed out and full of anxiety from the weight of raising them, parenting, and providing for them. Lord, I am tired and need your help. I am doing all that I can do. I lift up my stress and anxiety of raising my kids to you. I cannot do it without you. I come before your throne and ask you to refresh and strengthen me for the task of raising my kids on every level. I bind every demonic agenda and generational curses that are affecting my ability to be an effective parent. I rebuke every relationship in our lives that would cause them to go astray. Keep them Lord in your loving hands. I pray for wisdom to obtain the finances I need to provide for them. I pray for favor and open doors for all the things they need. I surrender myself to your will. I break off every curse of failing in school, incarceration, drug uses, sexual immorality, addiction, social media misuse, and habit that is ungodly. I pray for the fire of the Holy Ghost to sweep through my home to minister salvation to each of my kids. Deliver me from the stress fear and concern I have. I don't receive the tormenting thoughts of being overwhelmed. I receive the victory I have in Christ Jesus that my family is sanctified and set apart for a good work in you. Give me the time I need daily to pray, seek your face and get spiritual refreshed for the battles ahead. You are my God.

31

I run to you for strengths and power. I am redeemed. Put a new song in my heart. I thank you for deliverance from stress. Give me a peace in the storm now that surpass all understanding Lord. I thank you for that peace. You are the author and finisher of my faith. I pray for my faith to be strengthened to believe you for every need my family has that it will be met spirit, soul, and body. I bless my children. Thank you, Jesus, for the blessing over my children. Keep them from gangs, bad people, criminal activities, drugs, immoral life, false religions, and ungodliness. Long live, my children in you Lord Jesus. Keep them safe and let no harm comes to them. Keep them from sickness, disease, death, suicide, depression, and legal problems. You are the keeper of my head and theirs. I exalt you and praise you for answering my prayers this day. Their future in your hands to open doors no man can shut for; college, school jobs, and mates. May they walk with you throughout their lives. I thank you, God, for what you are doing and going to do for my children. In Jesus name Amen.

" O God, from my youth you have taught me, and I still proclaim your wondrous deeds So even to old age and gray hairs, O God, do not forsake me, until I proclaim your might to another generation, your power to all those to come." Psalm 71:17-18

Aging & Grief

Jehovah Rohi, The Lord my shepherd. I have lived this life trusting in you. As I get older, I realize more and more that my life is in you. There are many challenges I am facing as I age. I come to you for strength and revelations. I lift up my health to you to keep me, Lord. As Caleb in the word was able to fight with the best of them, keep me in good health. Any things in my youth that that would try to affect my life now, I bind it in Jesus name. Deliver me from the sins of my youth that would decay my body quicker. Quicken my health to be strong in you. Break off any generational curses that would wait until I get a certain age to attack. Shut it down now Lord and let my latter year in you be strong and healthy. Keep my mind, my soul, and body healthy in you. Teach me the things I need to do stay healthy in you. Let your word continue to come alive in my life as I age. Lord as I see so many I have loved passed away. Keep my spirit and hope strong in you. The grief is too hard to bear some days. Nevertheless, I know you are the keeper of their souls for those who have known you. Strengthen me through the losses and help me to press on in you. May my days be filled loving you. May my days and years be filled telling others about the gospel of Jesus Christ. May my day be filled guiding this generation to follow you. I live, love, and move in you lord. I thank you for the day of my life, every morning, and every night as I live in you! In Jesus name! Amen!

"'I know your works, your love and faith and service and patient endurance, and that your latter works exceed the first. But I have this against you, that you tolerate that woman Jezebel, who calls herself a prophetess and is teaching and seducing my servants to practice sexual immorality and to eat food sacrificed to idols.: Revelations 2:19-20

Witchcraft, Jezebel, Occult, & Abusive Church

Jehovah Sabbaoth, Lord of Host and Captain of the armies of heaven, there is a war in the heavens. In these last days Father, there is so much evil that is trying to prevail. Jesus empower me to fight the good fight. Teach me to pray and walk even greater in the Holy Spirit and your word. Deliver me from the Spirit of Jezebel that has attacked my life. Restore all that damage that has been by the attack. I bind jezebel an all her imps from operating in my life. Put a hedge of protection over me and my family from any counter attacks. I pray I am covered by the blood. I pray you set me to free from witchcraft prayers and curses, occult activity, and mystic Christians that are flowing out of the wrong spirit effect my family. Greater is he that is in me than he that is in the world! I do not receive those curses are spells. I speak psalm 109, send them back to the sender, and pray they are saved in Jesus name. Deliver me and my family from any abusive and controlling churches we have attended. Every prayer against since we left, I break its power in Jesus name. Restore my family to a solid walk of salvation in you. Heal us from the abuse in the church of control. Show us the way to follow you and become a disciple of your word. Do not let the mistakes the church made effect me or family from growing closer to you. In the name of Jesus, we are set free and proclaim your name Lord of the host! In Jesus name! Amen!

"And just as it is appointed for man to die once, and after that comes judgment, so Christ, having been offered once to bear the sins of many, will appear a second time, not to deal with sin but to save those who are eagerly waiting for him." Hebrew 9:27-28

Suicide

El- Gibhor, Mighty God who saves, I am feeling lost and need your restraining hand. This has been a difficult time for me. The days have been long. I am turning to you and your restraining love to help me defeat and conqueror the spirit of suicide and death. First Lord I realizes my life is not my own. It belongs to you. And thou it has been difficult to press forward I know you are my God and my creator. **You did not create** me with **an option** to take my life into my own hands. I feel the pressure and push of very difficult emotional and unseen forces. I bind every demon of suicide, death, and depression that is taunting me now. I cast them far away never to return in Jesus name. GO! I surrender and submit myself to you. I resist the demon that they must flee. I repent for all my sins and surrender my life to your spirit, soul, and body. Holy Spirit come now and refill me with power, hope, and love. I bind every generational curse that would push not to continue the life that belongs to God. I do not receive you. Holy Father I call upon you now to take full authority over my life. Fight this battle for me and walk me toward the victory I have in Christ Jesus. The problems that I am facing I know they are not too hard to for you. You have all power. You are Alpha and Omega. You hold my tomorrows, You got me through my yesterdays. I can face anything you in Jesus. Abba Father, this day and every day, I seek your face. Let your word come alive. Reboot my hope and purpose for life in you. Hide me in you Jesus that I may dwell in safety from the tempter that was pushing me to walk away from life too soon. I want to finish what I started in you. I want to love my family and be what you have called me to be. Not my will but your will be done. I want to live the life you have for me. I want to grow and use all that you have placed in me. I resist the temptation to end it all and run to your throne for strength and life. I want to see you glorify in my life. I will live to see and grow old the end of this life when it is time and no sooner. I rebuke the demon from hell trying to temp me to end my life and become hell bound. I desire to see the days in you. I know the day in you will be better, prosper, stronger, and hopeful. If I have you, Lord, I have everything I need to see this life through. I am your child, and you are my God. My savior. My Redeemer. My hope. My Deliverer. My strength. My Lord. My counselor. My provider. My way maker. My hope for tomorrow. You are Lord my everything. I am encouraged and restored now to you Jesus name. Restore my joy. Restore my peace. Restore my vision and dreams. Restore me lord to love you all the day of life. Heal any chemical imbalances that would cause me to be suicidal. I love you God and thank you for loving me even when I could not love myself! Your love through your son Jesus is the path I take now for victory. Heal my soul and my mind. Replace the evil thoughts with your daily words, prayer, fellowship, encouragement, and hope as I walk in your Holy Spirit. I thank you, God, for deliverance from suicide and giving up. I thank you for giving me another beautifully blessed day in you! I am ready to do your will and live this life lifting you up! In Jesus name! I will live! Amen

"For by grace you have been saved through faith. And this is not your own doing; it is the gift of God, not a result of works, so that no one may boast. For we are his workmanship, created in Christ Jesus for good works, which God prepared beforehand, that we should walk in them. "Ephesians 2: 8-10

Racism

God that gives to all men liberally, we are all your children. I have been faced with racism all my life. The hatred and the injustice I have seen and experience are unbearable sometimes. I do not want my heart to be hardened because of the hate I see around me. I thought that the world had grown past the point of hating me because of the color of y skin. I realize that in these last days that men's heart is still growing cold with hate. Lord, I don't want their hateful heart to cause me to walk in bitterness, unforgiving, or resentfulness. I lay down my hurts and anger from the many years of experiencing racism and injustice. It very hard not to be angry, but I believe your will and your word is greater than I am. I want to please you and be a vessel of love. Wash away the years of pain and resentment I have in me. Take away the sting of people's hateful actions that has affected my life. Help me to love my brothers and sisters no matter what color they are. Help me to forgive them for walking out your love daily in my life. I bind all demons of hate, rejection, unforgiving, and bitterness that would try to take root in my heart. I cast them to the desert and the dry places. I desire to be like Christ and walk in love. I yield myself to you as an instrument of love, justice, and unity whether I receive it back or not. I surrender to you. I ask you to heal any other parts of my soul, spirit, and mind that have been affected by racism over the years. Teach me to walk with Christ. Show me how to reason and bring understanding to my other Christians that have been walking in racism. Deliver them from their blindness, racism, blindness, and hatefulness. Help me to pray for them daily as led by you. Show them the truth of the cross through Jesus that we are all in your kingdom. In addition, show them that you are a God of love. I pray the gift you placed in me can be used to heal others in my race that has been damaged by racism. Lord, if there is anything me in that would affect my ability to be used by you from the racism I have experience, take it away. Teach me to love your way even when I am showered by hate and injustice by my white brothers or the system. Heal my anger so that it doesn't cause me to do my will and not yours. I thank you, God, that my heart has been set free from the effects of racism. I thank you that I know who I am in you. No matter what other races say, it will no longer matter or take root. Though I may not see justice on this earth, I know that when you return, all of us no, matter what color will answer for our lives. We will all stand before your throne. I pray that I may please you by being an instrument of love, fairness, humility, justice, and patience. I will keep my eyes on you. Your word says during the last day that there will be nations against nations. I see your word happening. Help me to stand for justice and what is right morally. Help me in politic to stand on the side of what is right, and nota political party. Let there be justice for all your children, not just one race or economic class. I will pray for the leaders of this nation and the world. Do not let lies prevail over injustice. Let truth rise up. I pray you keep me and family to still walk as born-again believer no matter which direction the world takes. May your word prevail in every area of my life! In Jesus name! Amen!

Prayers for the Body
Chapter 2
"You keep him in perfect peace whose mind is stayed on you because he trusts in you." Isaiah 26:2

"And when Jesus entered Peter's house, he saw his mother-in-law lying sick with a fever. He touched her hand, and the fever left her, and she rose and began to serve him. That evening they brought to him many who were oppressed by demons, and he cast out the spirits with a word and healed all who were sick. This was to fulfill what was spoken by the prophet Isaiah: "He took our illnesses and bore our diseases." Mathew 8:14-17

Headaches

Jehovah- Shammah, My God that that is always present! I need you as a healer to take away the severe headaches I have been experiencing. Release me from the stress, worries, and burdens I face daily. My headaches are becoming the center of my problems. It is taking away my joy, happiness, and my peace. I lift up my health to you now that you would touch me with your healing power. Deliver me from the headaches I have been experiencing. If they are connecting to another issue in my health heal that also, lord. I cry out to for delivery from a headache and severe pain I have been living through. I bind every demon of sickness and infirmity of headaches that have attacked me. I rebuke the affliction on my head, nerves, and muscle, right now in Jesus name. I lay hands on my head now and pray for your calming healing power to take away permanent this headache. Holy Spirit releases your power on me to heal. I command also peace to be still. I do not receive this sickness Lord anymore. Release the healing power over me. Take away the torment and the pain. I thank you for healing me. I receive deliverance now from headaches. Touch me with your power that every vessel and nerve is restored to excellences Jesus name. I pray that I can rest and sleep peacefully in you! I am healed from severe headache by the blood of the lamb in Jesus name. Amen!

"Now in the neighborhood of that place were lands belonging to the chief man of the island, named Publius, who received us and entertained us hospitably for three days. It happened that the father of Publius lay sick with fever and dysentery. And Paul visited him and prayed, and putting his hands on him healed him. 9 And when this had taken place, the rest of the people on the island who had diseases also came and were cured." Act 28: 7-9

Allergies/Flu/Cold

Ancient of Days, God of all the earth. I come to you sick in body. I need your healing power to take away the *Allergies/Flu/Cold* in my body. Rebuke the fever, Lord. Restore my breathing, eating, and body temperature back to normal. Take away the congestion, headache, aches, and pains. Heal my sinuses and all allergies Lord. I ask you to deliver me from the all the symptoms and side effect of this sickness. My body is weak and needs your loving hands to restore it. I pray Holy Father that the coughing, sneezing, body aches, lost of appetites, and everything associated with this ailment with subside. Jesus, I pray that I can get the rest I need and sleep peacefully in you. Use this time as I rest, to build back up my spirit, body, and mind. I pray that you contain this as you heal me so that it does not spread it to any of my loved ones. Heal me quickly of the flu. I thank you, that no matter what happens in my life, you are always there and willing to answer my prayers! I have faith you Lord to rebuke this sickness and heal me now from this affliction now. I thank you that the rest I have in you as my body brings forth the manifestation this healing. You have healed me! I gave you the praise and the glory. Thank you, Jesus, for answering my prayer. I am restored 100% in my body by faith in you! In Jesus name! Amen!

"But I will restore you to health and heal your wounds,' declares the Lord"
Jeremiah 30:17

Hands/Limbs/Bones/Back

Everlasting Light, I seek your face today for the healing of my body. My _____ is in need of healing. I have been in pain Lord that has been hard to live with. I have lived in pain for a long time. I know that you Jesus took everything I face to the cross. You have taken this sickness to the cross. I have faith in you as I cry out to heal my _____. Whatever happens in the past that has caused this great pain I ask you to be healed now from that event. I have trusted in medicine, doctors, and the ways of the worlds. You are the great physician. I look to you for a miracle. I am a good candidate for a miracle from you today. I have lived with this pain for a very long time. I surrender my body and mind to you Lord for a miracle. Touch me with your healing power. Strengthen my bones and heal me. Heal me 100%! Take away the pain and the need for constant medicines that is also affecting my life. Restore my finance from this sickness. It has caused great debt. Because I have lived with pain for so long, I honestly do not know what day without it would look like. However, I have faith in you. I believe by faith that you lord can do the impossible. I call on you now by faith for a healing miracle. I will glorify you in the healing. I will let others know that You Jesus did this miracle. I stand by your word that says whatever I ask in your name you would do it. I ask to be healed right now in Jesus name! I receive my healing miracle right now! Thank you, God, for healing me! By Jesus stripes, I am healed! I am healed! In Jesus name, I am healed! Thank you for my miracle today! I bless your name! The blood of Jesus heals me! Amen!

"And there was a woman who had had a discharge of blood for twelve years, and though she had spent all her living on physicians, she could not be healed by anyone. She came up behind him and touched the fringe of his garment, and immediately her discharge of blood ceased. And Jesus said, "Who was it that touched me?" When all denied it, Peter said, "Master, the crowds surround you and are pressing in on you!" But Jesus said, "Someone touched me, for I perceive that power has gone out from me." And when the woman saw that she was not hidden, she came trembling and falling down before him declared in the presence of all the people why she had touched him, and how she had been immediately healed. And he said to her, "Daughter, your faith has made you well; go in peace." "Luke 8: 43-48

Anemia

Son of David, have mercy on me. You have been my healer. Jesus by your stripes I am healed. Your blood Jesus covers over all my infirmities. I need your healing power to wash over my body and heal my blood. I lift anemia to you Father in heaven and pray for a complete deliverance from this blood disease. The women who had an issue with blood touch the hem of your garment. Jesus, I reach for you. I reach for you power and your virtue that came through the work of the cross. Correct the malfunction in my blood. Heal my body to work as a well-oiled machine. Restore the blood in the body to normal. Fix whatever is causing it to be broken. I have faith in you, Jesus, be my healer today. Restore my iron level to normal. Restore my strength to my body. Restore my hair and skin from the damage from the anemic condition. Work your miracle in me. I reach for you Jesus now. Let your power surge through me and do a miracle in me. I thank you for the doctors, but you are my great physician. I have reached out and you have answered. Today I am healed in Jesus name. My body belongs to you. I am healed. Thank you for restoring my blood and body back to normal. I receive my miracle now! In Jesus name. I am covered by the blood of Jesus, that heals my blood! Amen!

"You restored me to health and let me live. Surely it was for my benefit that I suffered such anguish. In your love you kept me from the pit of destruction; you have put all my sins behind your back."   Isaiah 38:16-17

Generational Disease

Akal'Esh, my God a Consuming Fire. My family has a long history of sickness and disease. I seek your face today for deliverance from the afflictions and diseases that have plagued my family and me. I don't want to see another generation be bound by these diseases. Father God I come before you asking you to rescue me and my family from generational sicknesses of ____. Let your power, mercy, and grace deliver my family from sickness. Jesus you lived, died, and rose again for me to come to you. I petition the throne of God for help. I remind the enemy because of that work we are covered the blood of Jesus. I bind every curse, witchcraft, generational curses, demonic bondage, afflictions, and disease that is over my family now in the name of Jesus. I cast you to the desert and dry places never to return. I bind generational diseases and curses over my family 100 generations back. I pull down the strongholds over my family. Every doorway and portal that diseases have come through I shut it, in Jesus name. Lord Jesus, I pray you loose your healing power now. I break early death, schemes, and evil assignments over my family by the blood of Jesus. God thank you that you are a restorer. Restore our health, mind, and spirit from the generational diseases. Restore our finance. Holy One, deliver each member of my family from any lingering effects of afflictions. I thank you today you have set us free! Let good health and long life be a banner and lifestyle for my family Lord. May we serve you all the days of lives. Thank you, Jesus for setting us free! In Jesus name Amen!

" What has been is what will be, and what has been done is what will be done and there is nothing new under the sun. Is there a thing of which it is said, "See, this is new"? It has been already. In the ages before us. There is no remembrance of former things, nor will there be any remembrance of later things yet to be among those who come after." Ecclesiastics 1:9-11

Menopause/Change of Life

Melekh Hakavod, King of Glory! Keeper of my mind, soul, and body. I seek your face for comfort during this time of change. I am going through the change of life. Things around me seem as different as I have aged. I pray you comfort me as my body and mind push toward a new era in my life. Father, I am overwhelmed at times with sadness, anger, regret, and frustration. Help my hormones to come into balance. I pray you help my body transition into the next stage quickly and with comfort. I pray that all the adjustment my body and mind at make will be of ease. Help me navigate through my emotions, body changes, and health issue that are arising, as I grow old. Jesus, be with me as I learn the new ways to walk at the stage of life and put away the past. I pray for direction. Guide me spiritual to be an elder to those around me. I pray Lord Help me to stay fit eat right, and exercise. I oar that you calm den the hot flashes, cold flashes, and insomnia from this transitions into aging. I know that I am youthful. Let your youthfulness in me, Lord Shine. Help me to grow in the word more at the stage of life that I can be a light to the generation coming up. Strengthen my family as they endure the change I am going through. Give them patience Lord to walk with me. I am excited about the new things you are doing in life. I do not want to get weary as I grow Old. So father help me to keep a godly outlook on what is ahead. Take away the dread I sometimes feels. I thank you for letting me make it this far and I know you will be with me as I grow in wisdom and in stature in you! In Jesus, name Amen.

"But he would feed you with the finest of the wheat,
and with honey from the rock I would satisfy you." Psalm 81:16

Diabetes

Jehovah Rapha, Lord God my healer! There are no words to express the battle I have been in. It is a lot for me to bear. God you alone are able to carry my burdens. Jesus, I cry out for a healing from Diabetes. The doctors have been great, but I need you. I come to you now and seek you for 100% healing. I pray for healing today. I seek you for a miracle that only you, you alone can do. Jesus, I believe you are willing. I have faith in you. Heal me from diabetes right now. Restore my blood sugars level to normal. Touch my body and heal it of all the afflictions and problems. I need a breakthrough now. I want to be healed by you! I don't want to live my life with diabetes ruling it. Bring everything back in control in the name of Jesus. I bind up the demons of Diabetes. I rebuke diabetes and generational curses of diabetes. I rebuke the damage it has done. Restore my body. It says in your word that whatever we bind on earth is bound in heaven. I bind diabetes and cast it far away from me! I do not receive it anymore. Father as you manifest this healing now in body change my lifestyle. Help me to exercise, eat, lose weight, live and flourish in my health. Help me to live healthier. I pray the doctors will even be astonished at the numbers are dropping now in Jesus name! I am healed! I believe the Diabetes has been broken off my life. I stand on your word that by Jesus stripes I am healed! Restore my body. Lead me Holy Spirit to walk this healing out while I am still taking my medications and getting a doctor confirmation of this miracle. Blood sugar you have been healed by the blood of Jesus. In Jesus name Thanks you God for this healing! **Note: As God has healed you, continue to take any medicines and do those things you need to do as he manifests his healing through the confirmation of your doctor. Believe by faith you are healed! You are in a war. Fight with wisdom and with faith. Be led by God. Receive your miracle! In Jesus name!**

"Dear friend, I pray that you may enjoy good health and that all may go well with you, even as your soul is getting along well." 3 John 1:2

High Blood Pressure

El Shaddai, God Almighty. I am so grateful and thankful for all the battles I have faced, you have seen me through. You have left no stone unturned in being there for me. My heart is full of thanks and praise for your mercy and kindness. My body is in a battle with blood pressures. I know there is so much more you have more me to do, so I need you to heal me today. I am thankful for the doctors and medicines that have sustained me. Help me to live and do things I need to do stay in good health. I look to you for a powerful healing in my body that you would lower my blood pressure right now and put in me on the path of staying low. I pray for Father that you heal any damage done in my body from the high blood pressure. Heal my heart, my limbs, my organs, and my body's functions. I rebuke any heart attacks that would try to take me out. I pray for a long life in you in Jesus name. Lower my blood pressure now miraculous with your loving touch. Touch me your power. Heal me now in Jesus name. I thank you, Lord, for answering my prayers. I thank you for healing me. I thank you for lowering my blood pressure. I believe the doctors will be in awe when they see the results. I will give you all the glory. As I take the medication and do the things I need to do as you manifest your healing I give you the glory! I am healed and set free! I am delivered. The enemy is defeated. Bless me with a long prosperous life that glorifies you! Thank you, Jesus, I plead your blood I am healed! **Note: As God has healed you, continue to take any medicines and do those things you need to do as he manifests his healing through the confirmation of your doctor. Believe by faith you are healed! You are in a war. Fight with wisdom and with faith. Be led by God. Receive your miracle! In Jesus name!**

"Worship the Lord your God, and his blessing will be on your food and water. I will take away sickness from among you..." Exodus 23:25

Cancer

Bread of Life, my redeemer. Your word says you never put more on us than we can bear. I am tired in body and spirit. I am facing many fears and concerns. My family is trying to be strong but they are also overwhelmed. Creator of all life, my body belongs to you. It is in the war to live. My cells have turned on each other. I am in a battle to live. I come to you now for healing. I need to be 100% healed. There is no one higher than you in the heaven I can turn to you. I run to you. Jesus the word says you healed them all. Heal me now. I rebuke the demon of Cancer in my body. I bind the curse of cancer over my life. I loose your healing power by the Holy Spirit now in Jesus name. Come now with the anointing power of God. Lay on my body. I need you, Lord, anoint me with healing now in Jesus. Help me get through the treatments. Heal me any of the side effects of the chemotherapy. Quicken my body, my soul, and spirit to wholeness. Remove very cancerous cell in my body. I will live and not die! Whatever the medicine did not get, you heal and remove. Restore my body health from the medical treatments that may have caused to damage to me. I receive by faith healing body from all cancer in me. I claim remission and healing! Every strand I command it to go now in Jesus name. Wipe my body clean God. By Jesus stripes, I am healed. Thank you, God, for healing me! Thank You, Jesus, for removing cancer. I thank you father for loving me throughout this sickness. Give me strength inside to walk this healing out as you manifest your glory. I thank you for my miracle! Keep me from any recurring cancer. I will glorify your name. Thank you, God, for healing me from Cancer. In Jesus, name Amen.

"Nevertheless, I will bring health and healing to it; I will heal my people and will let them enjoy abundant peace and security." " Jeremiah 33:6

Kidney Disease

Gracious Father, healer of all! I need you to heal me. My health is not the best. I am struggling with the reality I may need a new Kidney transplant or assistance with Dialysis on long-term based. I am trusting in you Lord to get me through this. I need a miracle and a creative miracle lord to take place. I cry out to you for a healing in my Kidneys. I am grateful for every day of life you have given me. You are the only one that can fix this. I am thankful for my family and the doctors and nurse that have to help me through this. I stand on your word that says I can ask anything in your name, you will do it. Jesus, my savior I know in my heart you took all sickness and disease to the cross. I lift up my sickness to you now that you will reach down to heal me. Create a new kidney if you need to, do a miracle in me lord. Provided a donor for me with excellent match if needed. I am in need of your power. There is no one higher than you, my creator. You are a miracle worker. Touch me and heal me. I pray for you to give me new kidneys! I pray for you to heal 100% Miraculous. Break generational curses of Kidney Disease. Take away the disease and heal my body of all the effects this disease has had. Heal me from the effect of the medication. Provide all the finances I need to pay the medical bills that have come from this sickness. I thank You, God, that you have answered my prayer. I come to you by faith. You are my healer! I am healed now in Jesus name! Thank you for the healing! Thank you for answered prayers. Thank you for new kidneys! I am healed! I give you the glory as I watch you move now healing my body. Thank you God for my creative miracle. In Jesus name. Amen!

"But he was wounded for our transgressions; he was crushed for our iniquities; upon him was the chastisement that brought us peace, and with his stripes, we are healed." Isaiah 53:5

Breast Cancer

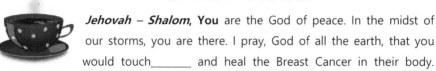

Jehovah – Shalom, **You** are the God of peace. In the midst of our storms, you are there. I pray, God of all the earth, that you would touch_____ and heal the Breast Cancer in their body. There is nothing too big for you God. Lord, you have all power to heal and restore us to perfect heal. Where the doctors end, Lord you begin. I seek your face Father that you would be a healer in this situation. Have mercy on ____ and heal Lord in your power and grace. Jesus, you said that the sick needs physicians... you are the great physician and healer! Work with the doctors, nurses, and medicine as you use them for your glory. But Lord, I believe you can heal without their help also if you choose, in your power! However, whichever way you decide to come, Lord, come in power, miracles, and divine intervention. Only you Lord can heal the body. Jesus, you died and rose again on the cross for us have the healing we need. It is by *your stripes Jesus* that we are healed. I bind every spirit of infirmity, every spirit of breast cancer, every spirit of sickness, and disease. I bind every spirit of affliction in Jesus name! Touch with your mercy and grace. Take away the pain; remove the breast cancer 100 percent. Take away the heaviness and depression. Remove every cancer from the body. Complete your work in the body with perfect health Lord. Heal the heart, soul, and spirit also. Help the love-ones that have been shaken by this event to know you even more as a healer in Jesus name. Strengthen the family in the midst of this trial to know you, Lord and savior. Father in heaven let your promise is fulfilled in the body by healing it of all disease. Lord provides all the money or the financial need that have occurred during this sickness. Send financial help and insurance that will cover all the needs. Show your power this hour! Show forth your love and divine intervention to heal with a miracle. And may you get all the glory Lord for the healing. In Jesus, name Amen

But he was wounded for our transgressions; he was crushed for our
iniquities; upon him was the chastisement that brought us peace, and with
his stripes, we are healed." Isaiah 53:5

Prostate Cancer

***Jehovah – Shalom,* You** are the God of peace. In the midst of
our storms, you are there. I pray, God of all the earth, that you
would touch_____ and heal the Prostate Cancer in the body.
There is nothing too big for you God.   Remove depression and sadness.
Only you Lord can heal the body. Jesus, you died and rose again on the
cross for us have the healing we need. It is by *your stripes Jesus* that we are
healed.   Lord, you have all power to heal and restore us to perfect heal.
Where the doctors end, Lord you begin. Strengthen the family in the midst
of this trial to know you, Lord and savior. Father in heaven let your promise
is fulfilled in the body by healing it of all disease.   Lord provides all the
money or the financial need that have occurred during this sickness. Send
financial help and insurance that will cover all the needs. I seek your face
Father that you would be a healer in this situation. I bind every spirit of
infirmity, every spirit of Prostate cancer, every spirit of sickness, and disease.
I bind every spirit of affliction in Jesus name! Touch with your mercy and
grace. Take away the pain; remove the breast cancer 100 percent. Remove
every cancer from the body. Complete your work in the body with perfect
health Lord. Work through the doctors, nurses, and medicine as you use
them for your glory. But Lord, I believe you can heal without their help also
if you choose, in your power! Have mercy on _____ and heal Lord in your
power and grace. Jesus, you said that the sick needs physicians... you are
the great physician and healer. Heal the heart, soul, and spirit also.   Help
the love-ones that have been discouraging. By this event to know you even
more as a healer in Jesus name. Work a miracle today Lord! Show your
power this hour! Show forth your love and divine intervention to heal with a
miracle. **In Jesus name. Amen**

"For he strengthens the bars of your gates; he blesses your children within you."
Psalm 147:13

Infertilities/Barren

You are God all by yourself. All power is in your hand. Lord, I ask if it is in your will that you open _____ womb and allow her to bring forth a child. You are God of all creation. You can answer ___ prayers if it is in your will. I pray for healing that if there is any sickness, infirmities, or disease that is afflicting my body that you will heal. Touch ___ organs and womb and heal them of cysts or any ailment. Jesus as you touched the Sarah's womb so touch _____ and restore her body to excellent health. As you restore and heal, if it is in your will also open the womb for birth and allow ___ to bring forth a child who is healthy. I pray this child is dedicated to you to be used for your glory all the days of his or her life. Holy Spirit teach me to pray for the pregnancy and the birthing of this child. Show _____ how to love, care for, and be a blessing as a parent to this child in Jesus' name. In___ body Lord, work miracles of healing and good health. I rebuke every generational curse of sickness, cysts, disease, breast cancer, diabetes, high blood pressure, heart problems, and circulatory problems in Jesus' name. Heal ____ from the top of ____ head to the bottom of ___ feet from every disease and disorder. Do creative miracles in and through _____. Let your supernatural power come and fall on _____ today Lord. I receive by faith your healing grace, release from barrenness, and excellent health. I even pray that as _____ goes to the doctor there will be documented proof of what you have done. Bless___, Lord, that ___may live all the days you have for ___in this life, long days of good health and power in you. Thank you, Jesus, for touching____ body and pouring out your power and presence. _____ is healed. ____ is set free! _____ is delivered! I pray the child is born healthy and provided for everything they need in this life. We are blessed and walking in your word and spirit in Jesus' name! Amen

"And they brought the boy to him. And when the spirit saw him, immediately it convulsed the boy, and he fell on the ground and roll" And Jesus asked his father, "How long has this been happening to him?" And he said, "From childhood. And it has often cast him into fire and into water, to destroy him. But if you can do anything, have compassion on us and help us." And Jesus said to him, "'If you can'! All things are possible for one who believes." Immediately the father of the child cried out[4] and said, "I believe; help my unbelief!" And when Jesus saw that a crowd came running together, he rebuked the unclean spirit, saying to it, "You mute and deaf spirit, I command you, come out of him and never enter him again." And after crying out and convulsing him terribly, it came out, and the boy was like a corpse, so that most of them said, "He is dead." But Jesus took him by the hand and lifted him up, and he arose."   Mark 9:20-26

Children Sickness

 Jesus of Nazareth, Son of the living God! My child is sick and I seek your face for their healing. I can't get through this without you. You are a God of all comfort. There is healing promised in the covenant I have with you. Jesus, you healed both adults and children in the word. Our victory as at the cross where you made away for me to come to you and ask anything in your name. I believe that you are my risen savior. You are a healer of all those who call upon you. By your grace and mercy, in your name Jesus heal my child! As a parent, I am greatly concerned about my child's sickness. Come now Lord, have mercy on my child. Heal them now. I will give you all the glory. I bind every disease affecting my child. I rebuke the sickness now in Jesus name. I bind the spirit of _____. I cast it to the dry places. I don't receive this disease as a way of life for my child. I rebuke generational curses over their lives right now in Jesus name! I remind the demons affecting them that greater is he that is me than he that is in the world. I lay hands on them now and command the healing power of God to come forth.

I loose your power of healing. I loose restorations. Lord, loose your ministering angels around them to usher in your presence and healing power in Jesus name. Father, I believe the blood of Jesus covers them. The gates of hell will not prevail against them and no weapon will prosper. I stand on your word! Holy God, take full control! Make your glory known. You alone are God over all things! Jesus, heal them now from this sickness. ! I pray for this healing miracle for my child right now in Jesus name. Have your way! Every infirmity spirit that is trying to take them out, Jesus contend with it now and rebuke it. I don't receive this disease in my child's life. I bring it to you to set them free! Shut any doors of sin that have caused this sickness. In your mighty name Jesus, I bless you and thank you for healing them. They are healed!

Restore their body, mind, and soul back to normal health. Supersede even the doctor's expectation. You are miracle worker praise you and thank you for their deliverance from this sickness. Rebuke anything else that is hidden trying to take them out. Remove it boldly Jesus from the midst of them. God, I thank you for this healing. Manifest your healing power in this sickness for your glory. I thank you for their recovery. I thank you that shall live and not die! I bind up the spirit of death. I loose a long life of good health over them! In Jesus name, I praise you for answering my prayer right now. There is no one like you God! I give you all the glory! In Jesus name! Amen!

"When Jesus perceived their thoughts, he answered them, "Why do you question in your hearts? Which is easier, to say, 'Your sins are forgiven you,' or to say, 'Rise and walk'? But that you may know that the Son of Man has authority on earth to forgive sins"-he said to the man who was paralyzed-"I say to you, rise, pick up your bed and go home." And immediately he rose up before them and picked up what he had been lying on and went home, glorifying God".Luke 5: 22-25

Paralysis /Walking

Lord of the Harvest, I am in need of a healing that only you can do. You are gracious and have all power. Where the doctors end, you begin Father. My desire is to walk again without any assistance. I desire to walk with the legs you gave me fully healed. I am grateful for every day I have in you. You are my strength and my hope. I could not have gone through this without you. I have faith you God through the mighty name of Jesus to heal my legs. In your word, Jesus healed them all. Jesus healed the paralyzed man. I come before you and asks you to heal my legs, back, spine, head, and nerves. Let me walk again. Jesus touch me now and strengthen my legs. Heal all the muscles, joints, nerves, and ligament to function again in unison. I give you free reign Lord to do what needs to be done that I may walk. Deliver me lord from the spirit of paralyze. I bind up the demonic forces that would hinder this miracle. I bind the spirit of infirmity on my legs. I rebuke everything hindering my healing. I send them to the abyss never to return to me! Father, I receive your healing power now! I receive my miracle now! I receive the restoration of my leg now that I can walk! I give you the glory and praise for deliverance. I am made whole in you. I take up my bed and walk! Thank God for healing me. In Jesus name. Amen.

" So his fame spread throughout all Syria, and they brought him all the sick, those afflicted with various diseases and pains, those oppressed by demons, epileptics, and paralytics, and he healed them" Mathew 4:24

Arthritis

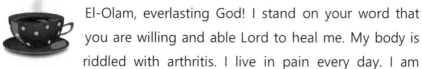 El-Olam, everlasting God! I stand on your word that you are willing and able Lord to heal me. My body is riddled with arthritis. I live in pain every day. I am tired, Lord. I am desperate for a healing. In the word Jesus, you healed all that were afflicted. I come to you now! I run to you! I need you, Lord, to take away the Arthritis that is my body. Heal my joints. Take away father the constant pain. Take away the swelling. Straighten out my fingers, arms, and limbs. You are able. There is no one higher on the throne I can come to. You are God all by yourself. You are the same yesterday and tomorrow, Jesus. You are my healer. Rebuke the spirits of Arthritis, Dropsy, Palsy, crippling demons, and paralyzes spirits that have tried to take me out. I am your Lord, loose your healing power now on me! I trust you, Jesus, to heal 100% my body. You took to cross, all my sickness and diseases. Healing is for everyone. Deliver me from any bitterness or sins in my heart that the enemy may have used as a gateway. I lift my heart to you to wash me whiter than snow. Create in me a clean heart. I bind up generational curse of arthritis in my life. I don't receive any curses spoken over me. The blood of the lamb sets me free. Thank you, God, for deliverance right now from Arthritis and all the other spirits. Thank you for healing my mind and soul. Jesus. I thank you for deliverance. I am healed. I am whole. I have the victory now over Arthritis through this miracle you did today! I am healed in Jesus name! Amen

"Blessed be the God and Father of our Lord Jesus Christ, the Father of mercies and God of all comfort, 4 who comforts us in all our affliction, so that we may be able to comfort those who are in any affliction, with the comfort with which we ourselves are comforted by God." 2 Corinthians 1: 3-4

Surgery

God of all comfort, forever present Father. I am facing surgery soon. I pray that you work with the doctors and nurses for a successful surgery. Heal me 100%, Lord. I need you to be with me Lord from beginning to end. Lord, be with me in the surgery. Take full control. Manifest my healing successfully. No matter what the enemy has planned to go wrong, I pray you destroy his plans. Take full control. Jesus be with my family during this pressing time. Guide the doctors, anesthesiologists, nurses, surgeons, and the hospital staff for my successful recovery. I bind all the works of the enemy in my surgery. I nullify his plans right now in Jesus' name! I will give you all the glory Lord as I come through this. Cover me with your blood Jesus. Keep me. I pray that any fears I have, take it away. Deliver me from fear. Take away the spirit of fear. Comfort me in this great time of need. I rest in you lord. My life is your hands alone. I confess your word over my life that I am more than conquered through Christ Jesus that gives me strength. I bind the spirit of death, destruction, and mishaps. I bind all chaos that would try to interfere with the surgery. NO weapon formed against me will prosper! I will live and not die! I come boldly to the throne of grace to find help and mercy in a time of need! I claim the victorious promises of God by the blood of Jesus for healing. Father God, keeper of my soul, mind, and body bring me through this that I may give you all the glory. I thank you ahead of time for taking full control that as your child I will be healed, restored, and come out of this surgery in excellent condition. Jesus, you are the great physician, I believe you will keep my healer, my God and me. Thank you, father that you will bring me through this surgery successfully. Let your angels be with me in the operating room. I pray I find favor with the staff. I pray I find favor with the insurance company to have surgery paid for in full. Provide the finances for the medical bills, Lord that I have accumulated. You know my needs are great! Thank you for comforting and delivering me from all fear and concerns. I praise you, Jesus that you are walking with me as I go forth in surgery. I give you all the glory and praise for a successful outcome from the surgery, In Jesus name Amen.

"My flesh and my heart may fail, but God is the strength of my heart and my portion forever." ~ Psalms 73:26

Heart/Lungs Breathing

Shepherd of my soul, I call on you. Everlasting father my heart and lungs are in need your healing grace. Heal my _____ now Lord and take away _____. I have fought the good fight, but the battle is not over. You are the shepherd of my soul. You war on my behalf. I am in need of a miracle. There are things going on in my body that the doctors can't reverse. Only you can heal. I bow down before you and cry for your mercy and healing power. In the inner parts of my body that only you made, come heal me now. I need a 100% healing that I can live this life glorifying you. My family has been faithful. Comfort their concerns. I bring this sickness to the cross now. Jesus fix this. Heal me. Manifest your healing power in my _____. I turn to you for greater strength and hope. I have faith in you as I cry out to heal me. If this was caused by any sins in my life, I repent Lord that I can be made whole. Take away anything in my life that would hinder the healing in my body. Lord Jesus by your stripes I am healed. I stand by your word. I open up my heart and mind now to you to be fully healed in my body. I thank you for the comfort you have given me. I thank you for each day of my life. Touch my heart, lungs, arteries, and blood now with your healing power in Jesus name. Break off every curse in my life. Set me free now. I worship you and praise you God for healing me now. My body, soul, and spirit are yours lord. Thank you, Jesus, for answering my prayer. I bless your name. I am excited about the healing you are doing now and give you the praise! I am healed in Jesus name! My____ is healed! I love you, Lord! Thank you, Jesus! In Jesus name! Amen!

"Jesus went on from there and walked beside the Sea of Galilee. And he went up on the mountain and sat down there. And great crowds came to him, bringing with them the lame, the blind, the crippled, the mute, and many others, and they put them at his feet, and he healed them, so that the crowd wondered, when they saw the mute speaking, the crippled healthy, the lame walking, and the blind seeing. And they glorified the God of Israel. "Mathew 15:29-31

All Disease

El Deah, God of all knowledge! You healed them all Jesus! There is nothing too hard for you. What is impossible for a man... is possible for you God. I lift up the sickness_____ to you now! I pray you heal me. I need total healing and restoration from this disease. I have faith in you Jesus to heal me. In the scripture, you healed all those who were in need. I am your child. I need you to heal_____ in Jesus name. I thank you, God for the comfort and compassion you have shown me. The doctors have helped, but you are the great physicians! Take away the pain, fatigue, and side effects that _____ have caused. Give e back my strength to live again in you. I will live and not die! It could be worse than this, but by your grace and mercy, you have restrained the enemy plans. Thank you for holding back the demons that have tried to overtake me in this sickness. I bind every demon spirit of _____ right now in Jesus name. I don't receive you! I rebuke you. Go! I cast you to the desert and the dry places never to return to me. Greater is he that is in me than he that is in the world. Loose your ministering angels now lord to restore and comfort me from this attack and sickness. Restore my body! Put a wall of fire around me Lord in Jesus name. I speak death destruction and burn by fire ever demon that has attacked my body, soul, and spirit. You are defeated in Jesus name. Father loose your healing power on me. You are a miracle worker and my great healer. The blood of Jesus covers me! The gates of hell will not prevail against me and no weapon will prosper!   I receive your anointed healing power now to wash over me! Pull down the strongholds and remove every trace of _____ in my life! Thank you, Jesus, for healing me! I proclaim healing over my life! I stand on your promises! I believe by faith I am healed! Reverse the curse and manifest this healing now! In the mighty name of Jesus, this sickness is bound and cast far from me! The blood of the lamb heals me! I am set free and shall recover all the losses from the sickness in my body and my life! In Jesus name! Amen!

"Come to me, all you who are weary and burdened, and I will give you rest. Take my yoke upon you and learn from me, for I am gentle and humble in heart, and you will find rest for your souls. For my yoke is easy and my burden is light." Matthew 11:28-30

Sexually Transmitted

Most High, God my creator, you have every hair on my head counted. As you told Jeremiah, you knew me in my mother's womb. You know everything about me. I have not walked as consistently as I should. Thank you for your mercy and grace. I have failed you many times. Father, I repent of my sins and being backslidden. I rededicate my life back to you Jesus. I denounce a lifestyle of sins and run to the cross. Jesus take my heart. Fill me with your Holy Spirit. I surrender to you. I am thankful that Jesus has made a way for me to be redeemed. Jesus wash me whiter than snow. Create in me a clean heart. Help me to obey your will. Help me to forgive myself. Help me to forgive others involved. Take away the guilt and shame I feel. My body is in need of a healing. Along the way, I contracted _____. I seek you for a healing in my body of ____. Rebuke this virus. Heal me now. Do a creative miracle in my blood, organs, cells, and reproductive organs. Deliver me from ____. I bind the spirit of infirmity, the spirit of ____, the demons of sexually transmitted disease, unclean spirits, incubus, succubus, and every spirit of associated with this ailment in Jesus name. Go! I cast you far from me in Jesus Name. I loose the healing power of God on my body. Cleanse me from every foul spirit that is not of you. Thank you God for healing me! I am grateful for the medicine and doctors, but you are the great physician. I am healed 100%. Thank you, Jesus, for my healing and deliverance. Remove bad relationships and set me free from them.

God, I love you. I pray for strength to walk upright before. I give you the glory. Thank you for healing me and restoring me to you! In Jesus name.

"Beloved, I pray that all may go well with you and that you may be in good health, as it goes well with your soul. For I rejoiced greatly when the brothers came and testified to your truth, as indeed you are walking in the truth. I have no greater joy than to hear that my children are walking in the truth" 3 John 1:2-4

Miscarriage

Jehovah Shalom, God of all peace. This has been a very hard trial. I am overcome with emotions. Help_____ deal with the miscarriage that has affected our lives. I am having a hard time processing it. I believe the child is in heaven with you. It was not time. However, it still hurts deep inside. Heal_____ body from the loss of the child. Heal the hormones as the body adjusts. Heal_____ emotions from the event. This is very devastating Lord. I pray heavenly father that you gird up my family. Bring peace and calm where there has not been any for a while. Heal the hearts of those who are broken from the event. The expectation of this child life was great, but you had other plans. Help us to accept your will. Heal my heart. Jesus the pain is great but you are here for us. Father of all comfort it may be a while before things get back to normal, but in the meantime let your peace and comfort be with _____ to ride out this storm. Heal the grief and despair. Take away any self-blame ad regrets. Let your love heal. Father give_____ a hug from heaven and wipe away the tears as you heal the heart deep pains. I love you God and thank you, that _____ is not in this alone. You are God all by yourself and faithful to comfort and be there for us now in a great time of need. Thank you, Jesus, for being with_____. In Jesus name. Amen

"Or do you not know that your body is a temple of the Holy Spirit within you, whom you have from God? You are not your own, for you were bought with a price. So glorify God in your body. 1 Corinthians 6:19

Obesity

King of Kings! And Lord of Lords! There is no one greater than you. In you, I live, move, and have my being. I come to you for help with my body, mind, and soul. Heal me from Obesity. I need your help to get my temple under control. I have been fighting this battle for a long time Lord. I need your help. I pray you deliver me from the medical problems I have losing weight. I pray I may lose____ pounds so that my body can be made whole. I believe that other disease will flee my body as I lose this weight in Jesus name. Heal me from all the complications that this have caused in my body and my life. I bind the spirit of gluttony, addiction to food, obesity, and spirit of death by food off my life in Jesus name. I cast them to the desert and dry places in Jesus name. I render those spirit uselessly operating in my life from today and here on out. I loose control, temperance, and desire to live and eat healthy over my life. Father on heaven set me from my hindering spirit, fragmenting souls, broken spirit, and years of disappointment in dieting that would cause me to fail. This is a reboot to lose weight with you Lord in control. I give my weight loss over to you to guide me, strengthen me. I pray your will be done in my body now that I lose the weight. Give me the energy to stay the course. Remove obstacle in my life. Give me a lifestyle of exercise, healthy eating, and healing in my mind and soul continually to get the result. I cannot do this with you, Lord. Teach me to fast and discipline my appetite Lord. I turn this over too you. I thank you for the victory and healing! I thank you for the weight I am going to lose! In Jesus name! Amen

"Beloved, I pray that all may go well with you and that you may be in good
health, as it goes well with your soul" 3John 1:2

Exercise & Good health

Yahweh, Wonderful God! I thank you for good health. I
pray you keep me in the years to come. Help me to
exercise daily, eat right, and live a lifestyle of good health.
If there is anything in my body that needs to be healed, touch me
with you loving power. I want to be whole spirit, soul and body.
Make me a threefold cord not easily broken. Gird up my appetite
that I eat in balance. Take away any gluttony spirit, obesity,
slothfulness, and generational curses that would plague my effect
to live healthy. I bind any addictions to food, drugs, alcohol,
habits, and ungodly appetites that are in my life. I loose
temperance, self-control, focus, and renewed purpose of my goal
to live healthily. Lord provides the right exercise, gym, or workout
that is tailored to meet my goals. I pray Lord you take away,
apathy and past disappointment that hinder my progress. Renew a
right spirit in me. Provide the finance for a good gym or
equipment in Jesus name. Provide the income needed to eat
healthy. I break the spirit of poverty over my life that can cause
me to live unhealthy. I thank you for the new goals and new
vision. I thank you Jesus for strengthen me to persevere in you. I
give you all the praise and glory for a lifestyle of healthy living! In
Jesus name! Amen! Write goal here:

_____

_____

_____

_____

"Blessed are those who hunger and thirst for righteousness, for they shall be satisfied. " Mathew 5:6

Medical insurance/Medical bills

Jehovah Jireh, my provider! You provide all my needs according to your riches and glory. There is no lack in you! Jesus, you have been my insurance in hard times. You have been the great physician in my life. I have been through many storms. Jesus my savior you have seen me through them all. I ask you, Lord, to get me through this storm as the medical bills and insurance bills pile up. I need favor Lord with the Government programs, hospitals, billing services, and Collection companies to get my bills under control. I can't do this alone Lord. I need divine financial intervention from you. Rescue me from the overwhelming task of paying these medical bills. I bind up the spirit of poverty that would try to affect my life from these bills in Jesus name. I rebuke the spirit of worry and fear from my life in Jesus name. I pray for debt cancelation, reduce amounts, favor, and bills paid off miraculously by you mighty God. Lord, you ain't broke! You area abundance God. I have inherited provision from your kingdom through Jesus. You are able to lord. Provide me with the increase to take care of past bills, new medical expenses, medicine, and my home and family. Help me to walk in no lack. Gird up my family during this financial crisis. Keep their hearts strong and trusting you in. I need the amount_____ paid Lord and/ or miraculously forgiven. Deliver me from medical debt as you see fit Lord. I trust you. I am good ground for a miracle. And you are a miracle worker! I thank you, Lord, for canceling my debt, providing income, and give me favor with my debtor. Provide me with a better insurance that I can afford! Thank you, Jesus, for favor, miracles, and more money to overcome! In Jesus name! Amen!

Prayers for the Spirit
Chapter 3

"You keep him in perfect peace whose mind is stayed on you because he trusts in you." Isaiah 26:2

"As they were going away, behold, a demon-oppressed man who was mute was brought to him. And when the demon had been cast out, the mute man spoke. And the crowds marveled, saying, "Never was anything like this seen in Israel." Mathew 9:32

Deliverance

My hiding place and shield, powerful God! The word of God says whom the son set free is free indeed. Jesus, throughout the word you deliver from demons, sickness, disease, and strongholds. I pray for deliverance for____. Set ____ free by your loving power. Your words say that we would tread on the serpents and scorpions and over all the power of the enemy. I pray for delivered from evil for ___. I bind up the demons and stronghold over___. I cast them into the Abyss in Jesus name. I bind unknown entities and spirits that are attacking___. I rebuke them in Jesus name. The gates of hell shall not prevail against them and no weapon formed against them shall prosper. Greater is he that is in me than he that is in the world. Father restore now. Loose your ministering angels around___. Lord. Put the hedge back up around ___. I pray you send angels with swords of fire to fight now in Jesus name. Help___ recover the ground in their lives that were lost in Jesus name. I speak judgment, destruction, and burn by fire every demon now in Jesus name. God in heaven pour out deliverance on ____ in every area of life. I pray that____ surrenders to you and resist the devil and demons that they must flee! Set____ free by the blood of the lamb! I thank you for deliverance for___ now. I pray ___ denounce every wicked thing oppressing. Restore ___ from being backslidden. I thank you fill ___ with your spirit from the top of the head to the bottom of their feet right now in Jesus name! Fall Holy Spirit! I praise you Jesus for setting ___ free! Thank you, Jesus, for delivering ___now! Have your way Holy Spirit in Jesus name! Amen

"You keep him in perfect peace whos mind is stayed on you, because he trusts in you. Trust in the LORD forever, for the LORD GOD is an everlasting rock." Isaiah 26:3-4

Tormenting in Spirit

Emmanuel, God with me! My mind is a battlefield. I need peace that comes from you. Lord, deliver me from tormenting spirits that have been attacking my mind. I have endured so much in this life. It seems like some days my past, my present, and my future are fighting inside of me. I hear the voices of shame, regret, fear, disappointment, frustrations, depression, and hopelessness. There are so many voices. They are attacking my ability to function. I feel overwhelmed. Your words says my sheep know my voice and the answer to no other. Father, I need peace of mind in the name of Jesus. I surrender and submit myself to you; I resist the devil and the demons that they must flee. I repent for anything I have done that may have been a doorway to torment. Set me free! Renew my mind to have the mind of Christ. Cleanse my thoughts Holy Spirit. Wash me that I may be whiter than snow. I rebuke the spirits of destruction and rulers of darkness in my life. I bind all tormenting demons attacking my mind in Jesus name. I cast them into the Abyss. Deliver me from the enemy's hands. Give me peace that surpasses all understanding. Peace be still in my mind in Jesus name. Jesus my savior restore me to peace. I give all my burdens to you. I bow down Jesus and worship you. I cry out to you! I receive the peace of God now in my mind. Flow over me like living water and have your way. Peace be still in mind, it belongs to Christ Jesus. Thanks for delivering me from torment. Shut the doors and portals that caused this. I thank you for setting me, free Father! Renew my mind like Christ! I receive peace in my thoughts. I am restored! I have peace of mind again! Thank you, Lord! The enemy is defeated! In Jesus name

"All things are lawful for me," but not all things are helpful. "All things are lawful for me," but I will not be enslaved by anything. "Food is meant for the stomach and the stomach for food"-and God will destroy both one and the other. The body is not meant for sexual immorality, but for the Lord, and the Lord for the body. And God raised the Lord and will also raise us up by his power." 1 Corinthians 6: 12-14

Sexual Spirit/ Pornography

God that shows mercy and faithful father. I have been struggling with sexual sins, temptations, and immoral lifestyles. I come before you lord broken and tired. I am tired, Lord. Every time I try to stop, I start all over again. I need you to deliver me from sexual sins and impure lifestyles. Deliver me from pornography addiction. Deliver me from sexual addiction. I am sorry that I have sinned against you and you alone. I don't want to cause others to fall because I am weak. Forgive me. You do not tempt us. I repent of all my sins. I take responsibility for my actions. I rededicate my life back to you! I am sorry Lord. Come back into my heart. Holy Spirit fills me now overflowing! Deliver me from all evil. I bind the demons of sexual sin, whoredom, incubus, succubus, pornography, and lust in Jesus name. I cast them to the desert and dry places now in Jesus name! Break off any generational curses of sexual immorally, bastard spirits, lust, and fornication off my life in Jesus name. As David cried out, I cry out to washed and cleansed by your spirit. Create in me a clean heart. Jesus give me the desire to live holy for you. Restore my body as the temple of Holy Spirit. Teach the biblical truths of sexuality. Make me holy, as you are Holy Father! Remove relationships, sexual objects, books, and covenant I have made with immortality. Set me free. Close the entranceway to those sins in my life. Lord remove all obstacles. Teach me your ways! I desire to walk virtuous. I can't do this alone. I need you! Make me pure again. Thank you for setting me free! Thank you for another chance. All my sins are at the cross! Jesus has delivered me! I am free from sexual sins! I have a fresh start! Thank you Jesus! In Jesus name. Amen!

" A hot-tempered man stirs up strife, but he who is slow to anger quiets contention." Proverbs 15: 18

Anger Spirit

Jehovah Tsidkenu, the Lord my righteousness. Jesus, you endured persecution. I am having a hard time with persecution and confrontations. I confess my sins that I don't handle my anger very well. Lord, I struggle with anger. I feel so much wraths inside me. I am overwhelmed with rage some days. I need your help. Somewhere done the road it has become a lifestyle. I don't want to be like this anymore. My family is affected by my anger. I am sorry. I want to be set free. Lord, anything can set me off, Lord. Jesus, I need you! I repent of my sins of anger. I seek your face for forgiveness. I run to you, my refuge and fortress. I am angry because I am frustrated inside. Only you understand Lord, How I feel. I know it is not good to hurt others with my angry outburst. Holy Spirit, I turn my life back over to you! May the fruits of the spirits of temperance, meekness, and gentleness live in my life. Help me to have self-control and stay calm. I need prophetic understanding Lord. Let me be slow to anger and quick to listen and love. Help me to listen to others. Stop me from reacting in my flesh. Keep me calm at all times and walking in the spirit. So I don't fulfill the laws of the flesh. Remove pride and selfishness. Let me considers others first instead of myself. I bind the demons of anger, violence, and rage. I don't receive them. I pray for temperance and humility to rule me. I break generational curses of anger, rage, and violence off my life. Jesus, live in me! I want to shine as a child of God. I don't want to take any glory from you by walking in anger. Create me in the image of Christ Jesus. Help me to reason and understand other better. I will listen to your voice. I will follow you. My heart, soul, and will are yours! I will glorify your name in my actions. Thank you for deliverance from anger. Anger no longer has a hold on me. I walk in temperance! I am set free! In Jesus name! Amen.

"Love is patient and kind; love does not envy or boast; it is not arrogant or rude. It does not insist on its own way; it is not irritable or resentful; it does not rejoice at wrongdoing, but rejoices with the truth. Love bears all things, believes all things, hopes all things, endures all things."   I Corinthians 13:2-5

Toxic Relationships

 God of love, healer of broken hearts. I keep finding myself in toxic ungodly relationships. Lord, I have had so many people in my life that have not had my best interested. I am drained, Lord. Jesus, I know that God has his best for me. At times, I have not waited for God. I have run ahead of his will. Mighty God, the enemy seems to set people in my path that have an agenda different from yours. I need deliverance from a season of toxic ungodly relationships. I submit myself to your will. I pray for deeper discernment and judgment. Before I even began a relationship again, help me to be prayerful waiting on you. Help me to hold back my impulses and walk in Godly wisdom. I pray you remove right now every person in my life that is toxic. Break oaths, covenant, and soul ties with them. Deliver me from soul ties that I have that have been physical. Break sexual soul ties in Jesus name. I will remove every object or gifts in my home that connects me. Reveal it so that I can destroy them. Break the witchcraft, curses, and strongholds that have released on my life. I rebuke very twisted entanglement I have with them now in Jesus name. Deliver me from all financial ties and commitments. Bind up Lord, every agenda and scheme the enemy has planned in my life. I don't receive it. I rebuke every foul spirit attached to them and their family. I am redeemed! I pray you put a new spirit in me to follow and wait on you. I pray for prophetic insights and revelation to take priority in my life. Thank you, Lord, for setting me free! I will wait on you from now on for the right healthy Godly relationship you establish. In Jesus name. Amen!

"When you come into the land that the LORD your God is giving you, you shall not learn to follow the abominable practices of those nations. There shall not be found among you anyone who burns his son or his daughter as an offering, anyone who practices divination or tells fortunes or interprets omens, or a sorcerer or a charmer or a medium or a necromancer or one who inquires of the dead, for whoever does these things is an abomination to the LORD. And because of these abominations the LORD your God is driving them out before you. You shall be blameless before the LORD your God," Deuteronomy 18:9-13

Occult/New Age/Horoscopes/Witchcraft

Rock of my salvation! My deliverer! Lord, this occult practice of_____ has been operating in my life. I ask you to forgive for allowing doors or portals to the practice of ____ come into my life. I repent for walking in these practices as a child of God. Purify me, Lord! Deliver me from the strongholds of_____. I repent for using____ boards and ____ cards. I denounce the use of ____ in my life. I run to you. I have played with darkness and evil that is now trying to take over my life. Break every oppressive spirit off my family and me. I pray you shut the entranceway and portal that these spirits have come through. I ask you to forgive me. I repent! I rededicate my life to you right now in Jesus name! Wash me and cleanse me of every foul practice of _____. I need the power to fight this lord, teach me the authority I have in Christ. Holy Spirit fill me and be refreshed in me now. Take back any ground that the enemy has. Put me in my cal! I surrender and submit myself to you. I resist the devil and demons that they must flee! Fill my home and my life with your power. I bind all demons from the practice of ____ in Jesus name. I bind witchcraft. I bind fascination with the paranormal. I speak judgment, destruction and burn by fire all demons oppressing my family and me. Lord break the chains! I denounce all occult practices. I don't receive evil in my life. Create in me a right spirit. Change me now for your glory. Restore me unto the Lord's will. Restore my family. Greater is he that is in me than he that is in the world. I rebuke every counter attacks in Jesus name. The blood of Jesus covers me. I am set free from ___ in Jesus name! Amen

"In peace, I will both lie down and sleep; for you alone, O LORD, make me dwell in safety." Psalm 4:8

Sleep Paralysis

Sabbaoth, God my protector! It has been very hard to sleep at night. I have been battling Sleep Paralysis. I cry out to you for deliverance. Lord, the enemy is attacking me at night. I have been waking up in fear and battling unseen forces. I call upon you now for deliverance. If there is anything in me that has caused a door or portal to open to this attack, shut it lord. I repent of my sins. I rededicate my life to you. I surrender to you and resist the devil and demons that they must flee. Remove any spirits/demons attached to any objects in my house. Show me the objects that are cursed so I can physically remove it. Heal me from Insomnia Lord I bind up every demon that is attached to me or anything in my home. Jesus helps me to walk in the authority in your name as your child. Stir up the gifts of God in me to use as weapons. I pray for guidance from the Holy Spirit to take authority over the forces attacking me. I bind every demon of sleep paralysis and night terrors. I bind shadow demons in Jesus name.I command those demons to be sent into the Abyss in Jesus name. I speak judgment, destruction, and burn by fire every demon that has attacked my family and me. Greater is he that is in me than he that is in the world! I pray Lord that you put a hedge of angels around me. Send forth Lord your warrior angles over to my home and family to battle the unseen force with a promised victory. I pray the blood of Jesus over my home and my family. God protect us from demonic forces night and day. Show yourself strong. I bless my home in Jesus name with the presence of the lord. I denounce any activities in my home that has opened the door. I break generational curses that have cause sleep paralysis in my family 50 times back. Every foul spirit I command you to go. I bind witchcraft sent to my family and me. I bind demons of terror/ torment in the name of Jesus. Lord remove every watcher spirit that has been sent. Father breaks every curse over my family sent by witches, evil forces, and those in the occult. If there is any evil residue from any movies, video games, books, or the activities that released these demons, remove them now in the name of Jesus. Jesus my savior you died and rose again on the cross for me to come to you for help. I come boldly to the throne of grace for help now. Whatever I am fighting that I can't discern, Lord you contend with it. I stand on your word that you are my mighty protector. Cleanse my life, my family and my home of everything that does not glorify you. If there are hidden things about my home I do not know, reveal! I pray the blood of Jesus cover my bedroom, my family's bedroom, and my home/property in Jesus name. I loose your presence and the fire of the Holy Ghost to pull down every stronghold, every evil entity, and all demonic forces. I serve you notice now to every demonic force your power is broken. We are cover by the blood on the mighty name of Jesus. Go! In Jesus. Wherever I put my foot is Holy Ground. My home is holy because you mighty God is there. I take back the ground now that the enemy has tried to gain to destroy my family and me. My home is a place of faith and a refuge with the abiding love of Jesus reigning. The gate of hell will not prevail me and no weapon formed against me will prosper. I thank you Lord for my home I thank you that we worship and serve you here. I pray for your Shekinah glory to rest in every square foot of my home. I don't receive those paralysis demons anymore. My sleep is blessed. My home is blessed. They have no legal right to come back again. I rebuke and foil the schemes and plan set for any future attack in Jesus name. Thank you, Lord, for ending the season of torment. I receive peaceful sleep for me and my family. NO more attacks. Any demon that would try to pin me down or hurt me will be met with judgment and sent to the abyss in Jesus name. I am set free! I give you all the glory. May the blessings of God, peace of Jesus, and presence of God reside in my home daily. I bless your name Lord for your mercy and loving grace during this trial. I am set free from sleep paralysis. Thank you, Jesus, for the victory! In Jesus, name Amen.

"For his anger is but for a moment and his favor is for a lifetime.
Weeping may tarry for the night, but joy comes with the morning."
Psalm 30:5

Jinxing/Almost Spirit

Author of life, Mighty creator. There is none like you. You know my comings and my going dear Lord. My life abides in you. Lord, every time I try to launch out in faith something goes wrong. I feel like I am dealing with a Jinxing demon and Almost stronghold over my life. I come before and seek deliverance from every hindering spirit that has caused something to go wrong in my life. Jesus delivers me from accident-prone demons, jinxing demons, almost spirit, hindering spirit, and obstacles assigned for my demise. I need a victory that I can only have in you. I pray you set me free now. Lord, refresh the call on my life. Through the battles, I have gotten disappointed. I need the vision to be made a plan so that when I am attacked I can stand on your will for me. Speak a prophetic word in my life concerning my call that I can hold onto in Jesus name. I surrender to you and resist everything that not of you that would cause me to miss the blessing you have in my life. I pray you would rush in like a mighty wind and remove every hindrance to my success. Remove every hindrance to walking out your call in my life in Jesus name. Jesus thank you for setting me free. I pray for divine favor in my life, I ask you Lord for a divine appointment, and establish your will in my life. Bring me before great me in my call. Break the pattern of failure and guide me to success in you. Open doors that no man can shut in Jesus name. I will walk through these new doors. I will give you all the glory in Jesus name! Thank you for setting me free. Thank you for another chance. I thank you for renewed hope and direction. I will no longer be subjected to hinder jinx and almost spirits. I have the victory! Jesus name! Amen

" As for me, I said in my prosperity, "I shall never be moved."
By your favor, O LORD, you made my mountain stand strong;
you hid your face; I was dismayed. To you, O LORD, I cry,
and to the Lord, I plead for mercy: "What profit is there in my death if I go
down to the pit?" Psalm 30: 6-9

Vagabond/ Poverty Spirit

Jehovah Jireh, who makes a way for me! Lord Jesus, I have not able to get stability in my life. It has been hard to recover from the financial difficulty have faced. God of all the earth I need a home. I have been moving from place to place. Provide me with the money to set get a home. Open doors for steady income, so that I can take care of the expenses of a new start. I need divine intervention Lord. I feel like I am cursed. I do not receive the vagabond spirit in my life anymore. I rebuke the assignment this demon has had with other evil entities to keep me from walking instability. I desire a home. You said you would give us the desire of our heart. I need you lord to break this off my life moving place to place. Along the way, any spirits I have picked up from others homes that are destructive, remove them from me in Jesus. Father in heaven; break the spirit of poverty that seems to follow me also. Every time I am established, something horrible happens. I bind the spirit of poverty and lack of my life. I loose favor and provision in Jesus name. You are my provider, Lord. I call for finances from the east and the west that your angels will bring it to me. I pray for favor, open doors, restore my credit, remove debt, cancel collection, and intervene in any court action that would affect me in Jesus name. Thank you for the new income, new job new home, new vision, and a new start in you. I am glad that you are God of a second chance in Jesus name. I am delivered and set free! Guide my decisions. I ask for wisdom to be led by you in all things. In Jesus name Amen.

"Therefore be imitators of God, as beloved children. And walk in love, as Christ loved us and gave himself up for us, a fragrant offering and sacrifice to God. "Ephesians 5:1

Rejection

Wonderful Savior! My life is hidden in you. I have faced so much rejection in. My sense of worth is very low. I need your love and healing power to defeat the overwhelming feeling of rejection that haunts my life. Father, I feel so unloved and unwanted by others. Even in my family, I feel rejection. Jesus, I accepted you in my heart as my savior because I experience the greatness of your love. For God so loved the world, that he gave his only begotten son so that I could have eternal life. I want my life to be hidden in you. I love you, Lord. I thank you for loving me even when I cannot love myself. I cry out to you for deliverance from the spirit of rejection. Cover me with your love manifest your power in my heart and heal the hidden deep, pocket of pain from rejection. Go to the places in my I can reach Lord. I open up my heart and soul to you to set me free from the constant pain of rejection. Help me to know who I am in you. I am the head and not the tail I am blessed going and blessed going out. I am mighty in you. I can do all things through Christ that gives me strength. I greatly love by you, God. No one in this world can love me that way you do Father in Heaven. Jesus thanks you for being my best friend and walked me through so many hard times. I bind the spirit of rejection. I do not submit my soul to it anymore. Create in me a new understanding of whom I am in. Let this work be permanent that I don't have to walk in rejection anymore. Build me up where other have torn me down. I forgive them, Lord, as you forgive me. I receive the refreshing if you love me my right. I am set free from rejection, YOU are creating a new image in me that is like Christ. Thank God for new strength and new revelation of my self-worth. In Jesus name. Amen

"For nation will rise against nation, and kingdom against kingdom, and there will be famines and earthquakes in various places. All these are but the beginning of the birth pains." Mathew 24:7-8

Racism/Hate

God of Love, keeper of our hearts. There is so much racism and hate in the world. I seek your face Lord that you would help me to walk in brotherly love. I see so much division in the world. Jesus, you spoke about the last days here on earth that the racism would increase. Keep my heart from becoming overcome with hate. Change the hearts those who are operating in racism and injustice. I want to be used by you as a solution in the world. I pray for those in leadership that are walking in racism that you would remove them from office or positions of power. Block policies that are steeped in hate, supremacy, and racism. Help the governments around the world to reason together and lay down their weapon of arms. Speak to the hearts of those who called themselves Christian. Guide them to walk like Jesus and not in politics. Chasten the churches to stand for the Love in the word of God. Jesus let love ring forth among the church. Help the church to not be divisive by walking in politics. I bind up the spirit of hate and racism that has effect my life and walk. I pray that no path I take is hindered by racism. Remove things that would block my blessings. I pray for open doors, in Jesus name. I ask you, Lord, to fulfill the call on my life. I rebuke the demonic assignments of racism in my life Remove any hatred in my heart. I want to be a vessel of your love in a hurting world. God of love, we need you now in these last days to take the gospel of Jesus Christ to the world. Override the racism and hatred that is trying to take over the body of Christ with the power of love. Your will be done. In Jesus name. Amen.

" Now may the God of peace who brought again from the dead our Lord Jesus, the great shepherd of the sheep, by the blood of the eternal covenant, equip you with everything good that you may do his will, working in us that which is pleasing in his sight, through Jesus Christ, to whom be glory forever and ever. Amen." Hebrew13:20-21

Blood of Jesus Closer to God

Abba Father and the Lamb of God. I thank you for redeeming me. Everything I have faced, you have been there for me. I thank you that I have been made whole by the blood of the lamb. I come to you in thanksgiving and praise for the all you have done. I pray the blood of Jesus will cover all the things in my life that still need healing. I pray the blood of Jesus over my family, my health, my job, my finances, my home, and my purpose. Jesus, your life gave us eternity. Your blood covers us. The enemy has tried to take me and my family, but your blood cover over all my needs. Your blood covers over all my sins. You have made a way for me to come to the throne of God and ask boldly for what I need by your Son Jesus. I praise you for the work of the cross. I desire to walk closer to you God. Make me a vessel that you can use to glorify your name. Create in me a clean heart. Deliver me from anything that would hinder your perfect will being done in my life. Use me Lord for your glory. I pray for revelations in my life to draw me closer to you. Stir up the gift in my life. Lord, speak prophetically in life that I can hide the word in my heart as you bring it to past. I have an expectation for you to do miracles in my life. Draw me closer to you daily. Make me more like Christ in Jesus name. I am your lord. I am blood washed. I am ready to hear from you. I love you and exalt you to the highest thank you for work you about to do in me! I am covered by the blood of Jesus in all things! In Jesus name Amen.

Remember when?
Chapter 4

"You! Right there in that hotel room! God loves you, Stop what you are doing. Jesus wants to change your life! He wants to heal you" Christian TV Stations 1950-80's

Look Back...

Back in the day, Christian Television had a parade of ministers that was sincere about winning souls. Many of the greats are gone. There were so many testimonies of people who came to know Christ because they heard the gospel on late night TV when they were alone and hurting at 3 am.

Their testimonies in the 70's would involve a minister pointing to the TV and speaking to them. They felt as of the minister knew them personally. The message from the TV minister would provoke them to cry out to God no matter what they were going through. There was very little begging for money....they were begging for souls. Somewhere down the road, things have gotten twisted. We are on a new day. The last days.

But the Spirit explicitly says that in later times some will fall away from the faith, paying attention to deceitful spirits and doctrines of demons,
I Timothy 4:1

The healing ministers on the Christian network would encourage people to such great places of faith. There was scam artist of course. There were also ministers also who really believed that by stretching your hands out to the TV you could be healed. The following week on the same station the minister would read letters from folks that had gotten healed.

There were also churches that spent a great amount of time waiting for God's presence to heal those who were sick. They had prayer lines. People's thirst for God to heal was being met.

I Look Back...

I have heard similar messages before many years ago when I have been up late watching TV. I am a night owl. I would go to bed around 3-5 am. Back in the early 90s, my husband and I preached in facilities, prisons, churches, shelters, and colleges throughout Ohio. We were honored and humbled that God would even use us to share the good news of the Gospel with others.

I got a call from Glenn and Darcel Leonard asking to join us in one of the prisons we ministered in that week. They wanted to share their testimony with the inmates.

We drove to the maximum-security prison we were to minister at that week with a Christian Rap group that worked with us. Glenn was one of the members of *The Temptations* back in the day. He still performs with them on tour. My uncle Nate Fitzgerald had toured with them too. I grew up with their music always playing in my house.

Darcel Leonard was one of the lead dancers on the *Solid Gold Show*. A top music hit show aired every week. She was the Black female dancer with the long hair that draped every-so gracefully when she moved. It was exciting to work with them on such a rare occasion.

They flew in by helicopter. It was an event for Black history month. We were invited by the Nation of Islam in the prison to come and share the arts, even though we were a Christian group. Our ministry displayed the arts in all artistic disciplines as a vehicle for preaching the Gospel. The ministry was called *On One Accord*.

As a visual artist, I had also arranged with the inmates and the chaplain to exhibit the artwork of the inmates during the events in the hall. I loved prison ministry because they were always open to anything unique that God used to give them strength and hope. My elder Lavelle Roe who recently went home to be with the Lord was there also. He taught me and encouraged me so much about moving in the Holy Spirit

After we finished ministering the arts in dance, rap, poetry, and music Glenn and Darcel shared their testimonies. Glenn talked about having a cocaine addiction that ran thousands of dollars and more a day. *He was up watching late night TV* and he said the preacher ministering late night on the television started talking **to him** while he was in the hotel room. It was not the drugs that had kicked in, but he said God knew he was in need of deliverance. He said the guy spoke as if he knew he was in that room dying from drugs and hurting from depression.

He gave his life to the Lord in that hotel room that night. He said he was changed. His marriage was restored. His testimony touched the heart of all the men there. The men meeting in that prison were all facing life sentences. They needed a living savior. Glenn's testimony spoke to their hearts. The altar was packed with men crying, getting saved, and praying in their new walk with Christ Jesus!

A little Faith
Chapter 5

"You! Right there in that hotel room! God loves you, Stop what you are doing. Jesus wants to change your life!"

Gone another way

Recently, I've noticed some disturbing trends. Whatever happened to the types of penetrating messages on Christian TV, which had the power to point people to Jesus? The Christian airways are now full of Christian infomercials, finance seminars, politics, racism, lies, compromise, tricks to get youth and millenniums, secular teachings, and gimmicks. Christian are flocking to the conference to pay hundreds of dollar for a word from the Lord. Millions are being made paying for a word or deliverance from celebrity ministers.

If you are sick and seeking God on Christian airways to the conference, then you will find pills, prayer shawls, prayer blankets, bee pollen, Torahs, scrolls, herbs, health ads, prayer cloths, holy water, blessed oil, jewelry, and mystical objects paid by Christian promoters within the church. Where is Jesus? Most of the major Christian networks, some churches, conference, and pop up churches are more concerned with paying their bills and keeping you hooked to their schemes. Sadly enough, it echoes that state of the church worldwide.

"Let no one in any way deceive you, for it will not come unless the apostasy comes first, and the man of lawlessness is revealed, the son of destruction." 2 Thessalonians 2:3

Thinking...

My concern is that if I needed spiritual help, healing, wanted Jesus or was looking for a Christian message... I would not find the Jesus of the Bible on most networks at 3 am in the morning. I am concerned that many people that are hurting are just sending in "seed offerings" to keep these scams on the Christian airway. Let me go old school for a minute to make my point...

Smith Wigglesworth, often referred to as 'the Apostle of Faith,' was one of the pioneers of the Pentecostal revival that occurred a century ago Without human refinement and education he was able to tap into the infinite resources of God to bring divine grace to multitude Thousands came to Christian faith in his meetings, hundreds were healed of serious illnesses and diseases as supernatural signs followed his ministry. A deep intimacy with his heavenly Father and an unquestioning faith in God's Word brought spectacular results and provided an example for all true believers of the Gospel.http://www.smithwigglesworth.com/

Great Revivals

Over the last 27 years, I have studied all the great revivals, and moves of God over the centuries. There are some that I question, but most of them were real moves of the God in the earth. From the Welsh Revival to the Azusa Street Revival of 1906. There have been great outpourings of the Holy Spirit to reach the hearts of men and women. The revivals consistently took place before or after great events hit communities worldwide. Like the revival before the Civil war with Jeremiah Lanphier

Revival 1858

On Wednesday, September 23, 1857, Jeremiah Lanphier opened the doors of the Dutch Reformed Church of Manhattan. He waited in the upper room of the consistory building. Nobody came, until around 12:30 he heard the footsteps of a man climbing the stairs. A few minutes after that more came until six men, representing five different denominations had joined Lanphier to pray. The next Wednesday between 14 and 20 people were in attendance. The third week, the prayer meeting was attended by between 30 and 40 men.

The meetings were so encouraging that it was decided that they should meet daily. The next day attendance increased again. Soon they filled the Dutch Reformed Church building. The agenda was simple: They prayed for the salvation of souls. The economic crash of 1857 forced thousands of merchants into bankruptcy, banks failed and railroad companies went under. In New York City alone, 30,000 people lost their jobs. In addition to the financial crisis, the nation was gripped by tensions over slavery. Sharp dissension and even civil war loomed on the horizon.

In March 1858 at noon prayer meeting was started in a large theatre. Half an hour before the announced time, it was filled to capacity. Because the majority of the attendees were businessmen, they started prayer meetings in public buildings. The newspaper editor, Horace Greely, who worked for the *New York Tribune* sent a reporter with horse and buggy to ride from one prayer meeting to the next to see how many men were praying. In one hour, he could only get to 12 meetings, but he counted more than 6,000 men. According to some eyewitnesses, within six months' time, these noontime prayer meetings were attracting 10,000 businessmen, all of them confessing their sins and praying for revival.

 A landslide of prayer began. Other major U.S. cities followed the same pattern. Soon a common mid-day sign on business premises would read, "We will re-open at the close of the prayer meeting." In cities such as Cleveland and St. Louis, thousands of people packed downtown churches 3 times per day, just to pray. There were 6,000 people in attendance in Pittsburgh. Daily prayer meetings were held in Washington D.C. at five different times to accommodate the crowds.

The effects were remarkable. Many ministers began having nightly services in which to lead men to Christ. People were converted, at times 10,000 people a week in New York City alone the revival movement spread throughout New England. Church bells would bring people to prayer at eight in the morning, at twelve noon, and six in the evening. In Chicago, the churches had a waiting list for people who wanted to teach Sunday school classes. The revival spread all across America and pastors were baptizing 20,000 people every week. Baptists reported that so many people had to be baptized that they couldn't get them into their churches. So they went to the river in the cold of winter, cut out a square of ice and baptized people in the cold water! The revival spread like wildfire across the country.

The 1857 Revival is barely remembered today by secular historians, but it was probably the greatest awakening ever experienced by the United States of America. It was estimated that in the period 1858-59 fully one million people were converted from a population of less than thirty million. http://reformedresource.net/index.php/worldviews/the-hand-of-god-in-history/123-revivals-in-north-america-the-great-revival-of-1857-in-new-york.html

The Revivals were needed

The power in the revivals was to provoke repentance and restoration to God through Jesus Christ by the Holy Spirit. The revivals were used by God to restore the things lost through the church's structuring of the Gospel that caused it to become ineffective. God restored gifts and power back to the church. The revivals were used by God to restore things in the church that had been taken away that are in the word of God. Man-made religions can sometimes remove God's truth from his people. He touched the people, towns, communities, and churches that had no power, no compassion, and had lost the Gospel message of Jesus Christ. The Azusa revival was before the 1906 earthquake.

Azusa Street History

Seymour was born to former slaves Simon and Phyllis Salabar Seymour in Centerville, Louisiana.[1] He was baptized at the Roman Catholic Church of the Assumption in Franklin, and attended the New Providence Baptist Church in Centerville with his family. The racial violence in the American South at this time — Louisiana had one of the highest rates of lynchings in the nation — would have a huge effect on Seymour's later emphasis on racial equality at the Azusa mission.[

In the 1890s, Seymour left the South in order to travel north, to places such as Memphis, St. Louis, and Indianapolis. By doing this, he escaped the horrific violence aimed at African Americans in the south during this period. Though he would continue to face racial prejudice in the north, it was not at the violent level that he faced in the South. In 1895, Seymour moved to Indianapolis, where he attended the Simpson Chapel Methodist Episcopal Church.[1] It was at this church where Seymour became a born-again Christian.

During Seymour's travels, he was influenced by Daniel S. Warner's Evening Light Saints, a Holiness group dedicated to racial equality. Their view of a racially egalitarian church would influence his theology for the rest of his life. In 1901, Seymour moved to Cincinnati, where his views on holiness and racial integration were shaped by a Bible school he attended. During this time, he contracted smallpox and subsequently went blind in his left eye. After overcoming smallpox, Seymour was ordained by the Evening Light

Saints. Seymour then traveled to Jackson, Mississippi, where he visited Charles Price Jones and left the South with a very firm commitment to his beliefs.

In 1906, due to the encouragement of his friend Lucy F. Farrow, Seymour joined a newly formed Bible school founded by Charles Parham in Houston, Texas Parham's teachings on the baptism of the Holy Spirit stuck with Seymour and influenced his later doctrine and theology. Seymour did not agree, however, with some of Parham's more radical views. He developed a belief in glossolalia ("speaking in tongues") as a confirmation of the gifts of the Holy Spirit when he witnessed it from one of his followers. He believed this proved  that the person was born-again and could then go to Heaven. Seymour did not remain at the school for very long — he spent just six weeks there, and left before his studies were complete. In late January or early February 1906, Neely Terry asked Seymour to pastor a church in Los Angeles. Feeling called by God, Seymour took the opportunity against Parham's wishes, and moved to Los Angeles.[1]

Seymour arrived in Los Angeles on February 22, 1906, and began preaching at Julia Hutchins's Holiness Church two days later. Less than two weeks later, he was expelled from the mission by Hutchins, who had padlocked the church door shut due to outrage over Seymour's claims on tongue-speech. Without a place to go, Seymour began staying at Edward Lee's home, and before long a prayer group began meeting at their house. The group quickly grew too large, and it was moved to Richard Asberry's house. On April 9, 1906, Lee spoke in tongues after Seymour laid hands on him, and the Azusa Street Revival began. Seymour himself received the Holy Spirit baptism three days later, on April 12. Soon the group grew too large for the Asberry's house as well, and the weight of the attendees caused the front porch to collapse, forcing Seymour to look for a new location. The mission moved to an old African Methodist Episcopal church building on Azusa Street, thus giving the movement its name.

At the beginning, the movement was racially egalitarian. Blacks and whites worshiped together at the same altar, against the normal segregation of the day. In September 1906, the leaders of the revival began printing the *Apostolic Faith* newsletter and argued through it that the Spirit was bringing people together across all social lines and boundaries to the revival. Seymour not only rejected the existing racial barriers in favor of "unity in Christ", he also rejected the then almost-universal barriers to women in any form of church leadership. Latinos soon began attending as well, after a Mexican-American worker received the Spirit baptism on April 13, 1906.

From his base on Azusa Street, he began to preach. This revival meeting extended from 1906 until 1909 and became known as the Azusa Street Revival... The resulting movement became widely known as "Pentecostalism", likening it to the manifestations of the Holy Spirit recorded as occurring in the first two chapters of Acts as occurring from the day of the Feast of Pentecost onwards. Charles Harrison Mason, the founder of the Church of God in Christ, received the baptism of the Holy Spirit at the revival.

In October 1906, Parham arrived at the Azusa revival. After observing racial mixing in worship, he went to the pulpit and began to preach a horrible word that God was disgusted at the state of the revival. Seymour refused to back down from the doctrines of the revival, and Parham mistakenly denounced the Azusa revival as false.

As the revival went on, issues began to pop up that would affect Seymour's leadership. It took only a couple of years before race issues within white America's perspective were addressed. The race issue became divisive for white America. Other missions affiliated with Azusa began to open and drew people away from the main revival. Racial segregation quickly became an issue.

The spirit of revival spread from Azusa all over the United States, and many missions modeled themselves after Azusa, especially the racially integrated services. By 1914, Pentecostalism had spread to almost every major U.S. city. The egalitarian message was very attractive to many people experiencing some sort of racial division all over the world. The mission quickly spread all around the world: from Liberia to the Middle East, to Sweden and Norway, the Pentecostal message flourished rapidly and many of the missionaries spreading the new message had themselves been at the Azusa revival Seymour's global influence spread far beyond the missions.

Protestant Pentecostals trace their roots back to early leaders such as Seymour, and estimates of worldwide Pentecostal membership ranges from 115 million to 400 million. Most modern Charismatic groups can claim some lineage to the Azusa Street Revival and Seymour Pentecostalism is the second largest Christian denomination in Latin America, behind Roman Catholicism, and many African churches are Pentecostal or Charismatic in practice. While there were many other centers for revivals, such as Topeka, India, and Chicago, it was the equality of races message of Azusa that appealed to many converts. Many specific doctrines taught at Azusa, such as glossolalia, are still taught today.

It not a Black or White Things...right?

The revival movements were not based on race, economics, or the financial makeup of the communities. The revivals were moves of God for a hurting world. There were historically documented records of miracles, signs, wonders, and healings. There was a man whose leg grew back out among the many recorded miracles.

The Azusa Street revival ended when they tried to control the outpouring. Also, racism was a major factor. Some of the White preachers, who witnessed the events, later did not like fellowshipping with Blacks. This is a hidden factor for the end of that revival. White leaders claimed to have birthed that move of God instead of giving full credit to William J. Seymour, a Black man. They started their own school of the Holy Spirit that segregated the Gospel. However, the movement for a racially free Gospel from the Azusa Street experience continued.

Your own personal revival.

The reason I added the revival movement to the book is to get you to get back on track of faith on what God has and can do for you. You need your own personal revival! God power is still here for you today. It is important to discern what you have been taught and why your faith may be wary. There is a need to examine and really discern what is being taught on the airwaves. My mother used to say before she went on to the glory that you have to know Jesus for yourself. The older saints I have listened to over the years who survived the Great Depression and hard times in America didn't have TV, pills, or seminars. They knew God for themselves because of what he did for them. Their testimonies are about a God who is always on time.

During the days of Jesus on earth the bible was not written yet. They people he healed had great faith in him. " Come see a man, the son of God that heals!"

The songs of older saints came from how they got over with simple faith. We have lost some of that and should reach back to go forward with the simple gospel of good news. Jesus born, lived, died, and was resurrected for our sins for us to have eternal life with God and healing when we need it!

Evangelist Woodworth-Etters in 1880 began her dynamic ministry—despite the fact that she had little formal education and didn't start preaching until she was age 35. She had a husband who didn't share her call to the ministry and wanted nothing more than to stay on their Ohio farm. Even though few women were in the pulpit at the time, Maria didn't doubt her call.

She was soon dubbed the "Trance Evangelist," though she believed the experience was the baptism of the Holy Spirit or "receiving the power." During an 1883 meeting in Fairview, Ohio, Maria wrote that the people confessed sin and "prayed for a baptism of the Holy Ghost and of fire."[4] Fifteen people came to the altar screaming for mercy and fell over in trances. Even at that early date, Maria called it "the Pentecostal power," adding that "these outpourings of the Holy Ghost were always followed by hundreds coming to Christ."

"The power which was given to the apostles in their day had never been taken from the church. The trouble was, the churches had sunk to the level of the world and were without the unlimited faith that will heal the sick and make the lame to walk. She prayed for the return of the old days and more faith in Christ among the people."M.Etter http://enrichmentjournal.ag.org/199901/086_woodsworth_etter.cfm

The word says

In the Bible, we are to heal the sick and pray with the power of God for those in need. The cross of Jesus Christ made a way for us to have power from on high. There is more to being a Christian than just taking infomercials, conference, pills and paying seed money to everyone on the air. The infomercials of pills and health gimmicks have taken the place of tent revivals, miracles, signs, and wonders. Many TV ministers are pushing faith in products instead of faith in God who has all power to heal whatever we go through. I am sure they get a cut of the profits.

It is time to get back to simple faith. Believe in God again as a healer. Trust in Jesus to answer your prayers. It is time to live what the word of God says in our faith!

Take the Medicine
Chapter 6

You and your doctor

Let me be clear that if you are taking medicine, exercising, taking vitamins or have medical conditions that warrant you taking prescriptions for your ailment **do what your doctor or provider ask you.** It is good to stay in good health, eat right, and take care of yourself medical. Unless God tells you otherwise and has healed you 100% of what you are dealing with stay the course until you are healed. Wait for your miracle to manifest. It is by faith in God that we believe. Use wisdom!

"Beloved, I pray that all may go well with you and that you may be in good health, as it goes well with your soul. For I rejoiced greatly when the brothers came and testified to your truth, as indeed you are walking in the truth. I have no greater joy than to hear that my children are walking in the truth." 3 John 1:1-4

It is the doctor's job as a doctor to give you good sound advice and use medicine as a tool along with diet and exercise to keep you healthy. However, it is not the roles of pastors, fake healers, and Christian TV ministers to sell you get rich quick-product and snake oil scheme to get you unknowing to pay their lifestyles and bills.

It is the role of the minister of all types in the New Testament to preach the good news of Jesus, pray for healing, and edify the body of Christ. I want to be clear about this.... *I am not advocating not following the order of your doctor.* I am speaking to the role of those in power in the church using *your* health issues, your fears, your generational ailments, your money, your concerns, and circumstance with your overall well beings as a means to profit.

The role of the minister is to preach the good news of the gospel, teach, to heal with pray, pray, and encourage you to seek God daily. The role of the minister in the five-fold minister is to edify the body of Christ. It is not to trick you in your vulnerable state of health to buy into get rich schemes, give seed officering, pay for the conference, buy tons of products, false prophecy, and quick cures from their products, and take advantage of your fears and concerns. That is out of order. Your doctor is your doctor for the body. The natural body needs medical and professional help. The body subjected to God's power spiritual is the power that heals the mind, soul, and body. That is the gospel Jesus walked out on this earth.

"And he gave the apostles, the prophets, the evangelists, the shepherds and teachers, to equip the saints for the work of ministry, for building up the body of Christ, until we all attain to the unity of the faith and of the knowledge of the Son of God, to mature manhood, to the measure of the stature of the fullness of Christ, so that we may no longer be children, tossed to and fro by the waves and carried about by every wind of doctrine, by human cunning, by craftiness in deceitful schemes. Rather, speaking the truth in love, we are to grow up in every way into him who is the head, into Christ, from whom the whole body, joined and held together by every joint with which it is equipped, when each part is working properly, makes the body grow so that it builds itself up in love."Ephesians 4: 11-16

We all can pray...

"And he came down with them and stood on a level place, with a great crowd of his disciples and a great multitude of people from all Judea and Jerusalem and the seacoast of Tyre and Sidon, Who came to hear him and to be healed of their diseases. And those who were troubled with unclean spirits were cured. And all the crowd sought to touch him, for power came out from him and healed them all."
Luke 6:18-19

The role of the saints of God, ministers, and believers saved by Jesus in the gospel was too supernatural superseding the known medical issues by his power and heal. Jesus was the great physician meaning he supersedes the diseases, demons, and doctor's diagnoses with his power. He healed them all! That was a divine move of his power. We have access to that through prayer to move as he moved.

"Is anyone among you suffering? Let him pray. Is anyone cheerful? Let him sing praise. Is anyone among you sick? Let him call for the elders of the church, and let them pray over him, anointing him with oil in the name of the Lord. And the prayer of faith will save the one who is sick, and the Lord will raise him up. And if he has committed sins, he will be forgiven. Therefore, confess your sins to one another and pray for one another, that you may be healed. The prayer of a righteous person has great power as it is working. Elijah was a man with a nature like ours, and he prayed fervently that it might not rain, and for three years and six months, it did not rain on the earth. Then he prayed again, and the heaven gave rain, and the earth bore its fruit." James 5:13-18

We can be healed supernaturally without doctors as the Lord Leads and move in his power. The doctor can treat you, God can heal you. But to have a folk trick you into taking their products and paying seed offering to fund their venue is just wrong. That is a misuse of the gospel. There is power in the name of Jesus and that what we should stand on. When all else has failed and the doctors cannot do any more... Jesus is the great physician that can heal us and restore us. It is God love for us that he gave us healing through his son Jesus Christ. We have power in his name to be healed and to pray for healing!

Jesus Heals a Blind Beggar

As he drew near to Jericho, a blind man was sitting by the roadside begging. And hearing a crowd going by, he inquired what this meant. They told him, "Jesus of Nazareth is passing by." [38] And he cried out, "Jesus, Son of David, have mercy on me!" And those who were in front rebuked him, telling him to be silent. But he cried out all the more,

"Son of David, have mercy on me!" [40] *And Jesus stopped and commanded him to be brought to him. And when he came near, he asked him, "What do you want me to do for you?" He said, "Lord, let me recover my sight." And Jesus said to him, "Recover your sight; your faith has made you well." And immediately he recovered his sight and followed him, glorifying God. And all the people, when they saw it, gave praise to God."*

Luke 18: 35 -43

In the Bible, Jesus healed the man who was blind. Jesus did not sell him pills or a prayer cloth. This new craze in the church is not walking by faith but is walking in deceptive gimmicks.

The 90's produce "self-help" a gospel that has spread through many churches. The focus became "helping yourself to get healed" whether God is involved or not. Christian Psychology became a staple in counseling people. The phrase "God helps those who help themselves "is not a scripture. This is a quote from Ben Franklin.

If I could help myself, then I wouldn't need Jesus. I tried helping myself without him in my life. I could not do it. I needed his power, his word, his spirit and his love to get through this life. He has healed my body, mind, and soul more times than I can count!

"As I wrote in my book **The Next Move of God***, there were at least five enemies that were trying to destroy the body of Christ: the Jezebel spirit, the Absalom spirit, the   pharisaical spirit, the witchcraft spirit, and the* **pseudo-counseling spirit.***" Fuchsia Pickett – Stones of Remembrance. How Twelve visitation of the Holy Spirit Changed One Woman's Life. 1998*

I accepted Jesus in my life because I came to the end of myself. I needed something greater and more powerful than I to live this life did. I did not create myself; therefore, I needed my God who understands what he created, to get me through. It is spiritually very hard to watch the Christian networks push pills and gimmicks instead of power, healing, and deliverance. I am not sure how the church got here, but it times to go back to the cross and just believe. The just shall live by faith! We have a living Savior Jesus that is willing and able!

Our own personal revival is getting back to walking by faith. It is a blessing to know that all you ever need has been provided by the God through the work of his son Jesus on the cross. It is just a prayer away! Faith comes by hearing the word of God... not schemes or crooked agenda. God's word is life! It is in his word. There are over 40,000 promises in the word of God. Those promises are for you. As you find them out those promises, you can also stand on them. And even if you don't know the word of God like that....we are saved by grace. He still got your back in the simple prayer of faith. Jesus came here on this earth and rose again, for what you are facing today!

"The Spirit of the Lord is upon me, for he has anointed me to bring Good News to the poor. He has sent me to proclaim that captives will be released, that the blind will see, that the oppressed will be set free, and that the time of the Lords favor has come." Luke 4: 18-19

 There was a time when instead of being encouraged to buy prayer shawls, attend the conference, get life coaches, and pay seed offering, we were encouraged to pray for miracles...on our own. There was a time that if you had a need you were encouraged to pray for God to answer prayers without you having to **pay off** God first to get it. I believe that power in prayer is still here today! In the Bible, Jesus healed them all. He gave us the same authority to pray for one another. He still answers prayers. He still heals! We are in a time in our generation where we need a healer! God still is in the business of healing...spirit, soul, and body!

Where to go from here
Chapter 7

I need to be healed

I can't imagine Jesus passing out pills to the lost and conducting seminars on how to start a business. The gospel that we are to believe in as Christians is based on faith, not fear. It is based upon truth, not schemes. During the 90s, the church did get off into a self-help movement. The arrival of the millennium ushered in a time of, "Get it for yourself". The user-friendly gospel moved in.

The prosperity movement in the church on the cable TV encourages you to get things to make you happy. *But joy is* everlasting. True happiness is peace with God through Jesus, Christ, and walking in the Holy Spirit daily.

As America is going through such a hard time economically, it is the hearts and souls of men and women that are broken that need true healing, love, power, and hope. Maybe things financially or health wise for you may not change quickly. However, there is a peace of mind, power, strength, and hope you can get as you believe in the true gospel of Christ when it is being preached. The gospel encourages us to be dependent on God through our prayer life. There is peace even in suffering when we trust God. God is bigger than America. His kingdom does not have a financial crisis or lack the means to heal you regardless of what you have been taught. There is no lack of him. He is able!

There still is power

The new covenant gospel is not about money or thing, but love and relationship restored back to God. The power the enemy has tried to remove... cannot be removed. It just might not be in the church you attend, but Jesus still has all power! He can show up at your house, office, car, a prayer closet, and bedroom. Call him up!

"You can ask for anything in my name, and I will do it so that the Son can bring glory to the Father." John 14:13

Testimony:
God healed our son and daughter

Do not fear what you are about to suffer. Look, the devil is about to throw some of you into prison to test you, and you will suffer tribulation for ten days. Be faithful even unto death, and I will give you the crown of life.
Revelation 2:10

Our miracles…

We have raised two amazing kids together in the last 27 years of marriage. At the age of 9, our son unknowingly was crippled with Systematic Juvenile Arthritis October of 1990. We found that out later. I was pregnant with our daughter Jasmine. I had cysts in the womb as big as a grapefruit that was pushing her out. They said she might not make it.

We were told our son never walk again from an unknown disease. His body was in great pain daily and bent over. He went from strong-athletic kids to a broken child. We were told he might never walk again normally from whatever it was. This was warfare. Ramon and I both were delivered from the occult before we became Christian. We become Christians with the knowledge that evil is real. This led us both to the conclusion our son's life and our daughter's life was under threat from dark forces. This was war! We needed Jesus!

"Confess your sins to each other and pray for each other so that you may be healed. The earnest prayer of a righteous person has great power and produces wonderful results." James 5:16

It all started with him falling at school on the playground. We were watching him die from what he was afflicted with... an unknown disease. He would never be able to walk on his own. He had a severe case that threatens to take his life. He was slowly dying. We found out later he was crippled with severe Systemic Juvenile Arthritis. It had a high death rate. We were watching him die

The cysts in the womb with our daughter threaten her life. For 9 months, I had to be on a phone-in system that recorded daily contractions. I was having 6 to 10 sever contraction daily. We feared she wouldn't make it. We were watching both our children die. We had to stop our ministry, take him to of school, and learn to pray.

New Year's 1991

Daily he would have high fevers and was very sick. From October to January, we did not know what was killing him. We went to church on New Year's night at World Harvest in Columbus Ohio. After a week of going back and forth to the emergency room, I ask God that night in the church to just give me the name of the demon and we would deal with it with his power and his word.

There was a prayer line that night at church on New Year's Eve. My husband carried Jamile down the aisle for prayer. He could not walk on his own. He came back from the prayer line walking and holding on to his dad.

He was somewhat better. I knew God was not through. This week I would find the name of the demon and get to war.

All the weeks prior to knowing what he had, I would go into his room at night and hear the Lord tell me what the enemy was trying to afflict him with. I would pray against it. The next day when we went to the hospital emergency room, they would test him again and **quote the name of the disease God had told me the nights** before the demons were trying to set on him. I was hearing clearly from God. He was spiking fevers that were over 103 daily. We were in the emergency regularly during this time. I was encouraged.

Need the name...

That following Friday, January 5, 1991 when we took him to the hospital again. This time they kept him. The ran a set of different test. Many tests. The specialist came in and told us what he had. He was never to walk again based on their diagnostic. Systematic Juvenile Arthritis. But God had another place. The biblical name we found for his ailment was "Dropsy"...Similar to Arthritis.

"One Sabbath, when he went to dine at the house of a ruler of the Pharisees, they were watching him carefully. And behold, there was a man before him who had dropsy. And Jesus responded to the lawyers and Pharisees, saying, "Is it lawful to heal on the Sabbath, or not?" 4 But they remained silent. Then he took him and healed him and sent him away. "Luke 14: 1-5

From January to April before our daughter was born we prayed, fasted, bound demons, spoke, read books, the Bible, and stood on God word. We never accepted the disease as being final. We never accepted our daughter not being born. *Jesus Heals a Man with Dropsy on the Sabbath* **Luke 14: 1-6**

This story describes an amazing miracle performed by Jesus on the Sabbath, a healing of a man who suffered from a condition known as Dropsy, which causes an abnormal amount of swellings in the body. When Jesus was eating in the house of a prominent Pharisee, a man was in front of him suffering from this disease.
http://www.beliefnet.com/faiths/galleries/miracles-of-jesus-6-you-didnt-know.aspx?p=4

We prayed against all the demons, sins, and all curses affecting both our kids. We had a prophetic word from God that they both would be healed. We stopped attending church for a while because there was no power or prayer going forth. They had given up. We were counseled to just make the best of it by other believers. So we put the prayer and power in our home daily. We needed a living savior. Jesus!

"For the vision is yet for the appointed time; It hastens toward the goal and it will not fail. Though it tarries, wait for it; For it will certainly come, it will not delay." Habakkuk 2: 2-3

The Lord told us he would dance around the world and our daughter would be into film, media, and writing. We held onto that word. On April 25, 1991, that day our daughter was born they could not find any trace of the cysts. It was gone! Miraculously. God had solved one problem. He had moved. That same week our son got sick from the medicine. We took him to the doctor. They ran a test and could not find any trace of the Arthritis. It was gone. It was a miracle. The doctor said he had never seen anything like it and said it was God not him that cause they miracle. It was gone. From that day one on both our kids, God fulfilled his word in their lives.

And Now

Jamile was on "So you think you can dance?" 2005 season one finalist. He made it from the 100 tryouts to the final three. He won the show by popular votes. Since then he has danced all around the world. Our son has traveled the world dancing with major artists: Beyonce, Chris Brown, Wayne Brady, and Mary J Blige, to name a few. He has been on TV and in movies. He has performed with countless people. He is a success! He teaches dance. He is a choreographer The Lord had given us a prophetic word when he was crippled that he would dance all around the world and God fulfilled it

Jasmine starting managing Jamile when she was 14 when he was on SYTYCD. She handled all his social media and films. She finished high school on a fast track in three years. She graduated from college on a fast track in three years.

He gave a word for our daughter would be film and media. She has worked within the advertisement. She has worked for major companies, magazines, and social media outlet. Including The Travel channel and Coke Cola. She is a film/video maker, digital content, and graphic designer. God word was fulfilled! They both are alive and a success! We are proud of them both. We prayed and sought the Lord's face. It was our miracle. Ramon and I stood on our faith. It was a building block for the many struggles to come in the 27 years of marriage. It as has been warfare from day one. God has been faithful every day in showing us how to war and pray for our family. To God is all the glory!

Be strong and courageous. Do not fear or be in dread of them, for it is the Lord your God who goes with you. He will not leave you or forsake you.

Deuteronomy 31:6

A Faith Walk for Healing
Chapter 8

Know him

I was told many years ago by my Elder Lavelle Roe I **to always know your salvation**. I have read the word that there was coming a time when the word of God would be hard to find and dry up because men's hearts would become cold. That day is here it seems. I have seen more schemes and corrupt teachings that are being presented as the gospel truth. Know your salvation...

Knowing your salvation mean knowing what the birth, life, death, and resurrection of Jesus mean in your covenant with God. Through Jesus Christ and the worked on the cross, we have access to God. We are restored to him by accepting his son in our hearts. We are redeemed. We are a peace with our walk with God. We are in fellowship with Jesus through the baptism and infilling of his spirit in our life. We are kingdom citizen. There is so much embodied in knowing what Jesus.

It yours

In that reality of accepting Jesus Christ, we are restored. Jesus restored everything loss from mankind from the fall of Adam. He restored us to God through his birth, life, death, and being our risen savior.

The Scriptures tell us, "The first man, Adam, became a living person." But the last Adam–that is, Christ–is a life-giving Spirit."
I Corinthians 15:45

It is our faith and belief in the work on the cross that Jesus through his blood gave us restored fellowship broken through Adam and Eve. Jesus gave us life eternal. In that, life there is healing.

Now may the God of peace who brought again from the dead our Lord Jesus, the great shepherd of the sheep, by the blood of the eternal covenant, equip you with everything good that you may do his will, working in us that which is pleasing in his sight, through Jesus Christ, to whom be glory forever and ever. Amen." Hebrew 13:20

The real thing

If you look back through the Bible many things that happen in the Old Testament were counterfeit of the real thing. There were sorcerers that did magic, false prophets, false miracles false gods and false power. The power of darkness knew the real thing was coming. Evil's attempts to deceive the children of God was to take their off the promise God gave of the living Savior Jesus through the Old Testament as promise through David.

There were also a real miracle, real prophets, and the real power of God. This was God loving grace showing them he did have all power still and more was to come through Jesus. This kept their faith in him and his promises to bring forth a living savior.

"He was despised and rejected by men; a man of sorrows, and acquainted with grief, and as one from whom men hide their faces he was despised, and we esteemed him not. Surely, he has borne our grief and carried our sorrows; yet we esteemed him stricken, smitten by God, and afflicted. But he was wounded for our transgressions he was crushed for our iniquities; upon him was the chastisement that brought us peace, and with his stripes, we are healed."
Isaiah 53:3-5

An also the difference in the Old Testament was the access to it God's by the people was in the law and interaction through principles. We have the law of the spirit through the baptism of Holy Ghost by the work of Jesus on the cross. A new covenant, a better covenant!

"For the law of the Spirit of life has set you free in Christ Jesus from the law of sin and death." Roman 8:2

Way back

In the Old Testament those who operated in the things of God operated by the power of God hovering over them or dwelling with them through interaction. In the temple, the priest interacted with God for the people. The prophet gave them God's word. Angels appeared to guide them; the heaven used every way of communication you can think of except the indwelling of the Holy Spirit. That did not happen until Jesus came on the scenes, that the Holy Spirit was present in the Old Testament and active. Jesus was the first to be filled! God's beloved son!

The sorcerer and false prophet operated in evil power that counterfeited God's real power. This power of evil was in the operating in the atmosphere that led them the false prophets and others. There were witches, wizard, and prophets that were under the power of other false gods and darkness.

"When you enter the land the Lord your God is giving you, do not learn to imitate the detestable ways of the nations there... Let no one be found among you who sacrifices their son or daughter in the fire, who practices divination or sorcery, interprets omens, engages in witchcraft, or casts spells, or who is a medium or spirits or who consults the dead. Anyone who does these things is detestable to the LORD; because of these same detestable practices the Lord your God will drive out those nations before you." Deuteronomy 18 9-12

In the passage, Deuteronomy 18 God never said that this thing *didn't happen*. In fact, He stated that they should not be a part of it and what will happen to those who practice these things. These practices were a way that people got results outside of God for healing, deliverance, issues of life, family matters, and false power for their circumstances to be resolves. It took people eye off on

God and put their eyes on false gods. That is why such great judgment fell on the children of God in the Old Testament. God was preserving them for the entrance of Jesus Christ in as seen in the gospel of Matthew.

The fake and there is the real

Today many fake minister and Christian celebrities can take believer's eye off God and put their eyes on them. People flock to many counterfeit prophets and events looking for God but finding imitations and no anointing. It has gotten to the place where the anointing is faked so much that people can't discern the real thing. The minister and false prophets overpower the service, provoke fear if they are questioned, and encourage an atmosphere of compromise over the believers attending. The standard is dropped so low that no one is discerning that is emotional hype with no powers. Very few are getting out of wheelchairs, very few are healed, and all the "forced praises" began to fake a move of God. It has become the standard.

"Woe unto them! For they have gone in the way of Cain, and ran greedily after the error of Balaam for reward, and perished in the gainsaying of Core. These are spots in your feasts of charity, when they feast on you, feeding themselves without fear: clouds without water, carried about of winds; trees whose fruit withered, without fruit, twice dead, plucked up by the roots; Raging waves of the sea, foaming out their own shame; wandering stars, to whom is reserved the blackness of darkness forever." Jude 1: 11-13

This is important to note because if you are exposed in Christendom to false teachings, fake minister, Christian witches, and fake healing lines pushing people down, you can discern what is real by knowing that the counterfeit does exist. Walk in discernment!

There **are real** prophets, teachers, pastors, evangelists, and apostles who are truly walking and doing God's work. They are unsung heroes that have committed their lives to God at any cost. You may not find them in a mega church. They may be on YouTube teaching from their homes, holding a meeting in hotels, or small churches. You may find them teaching bible studies in large unknown churches or on the job.

They may be sitting in megachurch praying for the lost and sick, but not allowed to the minister. They may be banned from churches. They might be doing the work of the gospel in the marketplace faithful seeking for God to use them.

God still has an army that is faithfully serving him and walking in his power to heal with miracles. You might be that soldier God has called to walk in his power and teach his word. Be faithful in your call. Pray for those who are sincerely walking in God's will in these last days. The real power of God is still moving!

Sin made it complicated...

The men and women of God in the Old Testament flowed in the righteousness of God in their lives by his power and presence through **external means and prayer.** A good example is a process what folks had to do to communion with God in the Old Testament. They prayed, but there also was:

sacrificing of animals, entering into the holiness of holiness, temples worship, fasting, crying out, and priest petitioning God on behalf of the people and giving offerings to name of few.

Prayer was a vehicle for ushering up the request to God in their relationship with him. They did not have the indwelling Holy Spirit, but he was still with them and dwelling with them daily. He answered prayers! We serve a faithful God. The sin in the garden made it complicated, but God was still faithful.

He made a way

Jesus made a way for us through salvation so we don't have to give sacrifices or offering to have God's power and restore relationship in our lives. He became our sacrifice. We have a new covenant through Jesus Christ that gives us a direct connection with him by the Holy Spirit abiding in us as we accept Jesus Christ as Lord and savior. We get baptizes in the Holy Spirit and have the indwelling power needed to pray, walk, and fellowship with God through Jesus Christ. In our prayers, we can touch heaven and earth at the same time and never leave the room! We have access to a holy and faithful God!

Now with that being said in the Old Testament everything that needed to be restored through our relationship with God was restored through Jesus to us by accepting his son. Starting with fellowship with God by salvation through Jesus Christ. From there God gave us access to healing, miracles, powers, and communion with him through Jesus and the Holy Spirit. We have access to the real God of the universe through Jesus Christ. We don't need psychics, sorcery, wizards, witches, and dark powers to walk with God to obtain miracles, healing, or power. We have the real thing.

"...the scroll of the prophet Isaiah was handed to Him. Unrolling it, He found the place where it was written: "The Spirit of the Lord is upon me, for he has anointed me to bring Good News to the poor. He has sent me to proclaim that captives will be released, that the blind will see, that the oppressed will be set free, to proclaim the year of the Lord's favor."...
Luke 4: 17-19

Why am I going over this?

The reason in this book I am going over this so you know your place in God to ask as you pray the prayers in this book. I am cleaning house in the way so that the word of God and his will can shine into your circumstance. Your faith will rise to a great height for your healing in knowing **who and what you** have access to in your walk as a believer! You are under the blood of Christ!

Knowledge is power in Christ Jesus! I am going over all of this because that need to really know and believe he can heal you is not going to come from the prayers in this book, but from your simple child-like faith in knowing that you can ask God. He will answer. Just ask.

"Truly, truly, I say to you, whoever believes in me will also do the works that I do, and greater works than these will he do because I am going to the Father. Whatever you ask in my name, this I will do, that

the Father may be glorified in the Son. If you ask me anything in my name, I will do it. John 14:12-13

It is your muster seed faith that you can go to God because you are his child through adoption by accepting Jesus his son. You are restored. You are his. You have a right to ask you father in heaven for help! It is important to know your authority and place in his kingdom... you are his. You abide by him. He abides in you. He has your best interest at heart! That why he gave us Jesus!

Obama Care......Jesus Care!

In our salvation, Jesus has made a way to come to him as we are cover by his blood and have a covenant with him as God's children through the work on the cross. Everything we need... Jesus made a way. There is Obama Care. We have Jesus Care! As we have faith in what Jesus did than we can boldly pray for what we need, worship him, expect miracles, expect to heal, expect answered prayers, and fellowship with God in when our brokenness. We are redeemed! Jesus has made a way...Jesus Care!

"Just believe that I am in the Father and the Father is in me. Or at least believe because of the work you have seen me do. I tell you the truth, anyone who believes in me will do the same works I have done, and even greater works because I am going to be with the Father. You can ask for anything in my name, and I will do it so that the Son can bring glory to the Father." John 14:11-13

Have Faith in Him!
Chapter 9

"And when they heard it, they lifted their voices together to God and said, Sovereign Lord, who made the heaven and the earth and the sea and everything in them, who through the mouth of our father David, your servant,⁴ said by the Holy Spirit," Acts 34:24

The God we serve is sovereign. He is in control of all things. He loves us and gave his son for us to have eternal life we are restored. He has all power!

sov·er·eign·ty - supreme power or authority.

Our God is Sovereign! Because of that, we are redeemed. We are abiding in him. We are beloved by the beloved. We have power in him. We access to his power through Jesus. We have heaven's ear. We have fellowship with his spirit. We have hope. We have faith. We have guidance. We have his presence.

We have an intercessor called Jesus. We have a way out. We have healed. We have miracles. We have gifts of the spirit. We have the fruit of the spirit. We have Angels. We have a prayer around the world from other believers. We have intercessions that we can do. We have God's hand on us. We have God's word in us. We have the word of God to guide us. We have the whole armor of God put us.

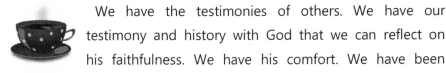 We have the testimonies of others. We have our testimony and history with God that we can reflect on his faithfulness. We have his comfort. We have been used to comfort others.

We have a God that rules the universe. We have a God that owns the whole earth. We have God that has all power he uses to keep us. We have a God that has made us the apple of his eye. We have a God that is a mighty warrior. We have a God that is in control of the ocean, seas, and the winds.

We have a God that is a consuming fire. We have a God that is the light in the universe. We have a God that holds the whole earth in his hands. He holds the stars in place. We have a God that has power over the body and the power of the soul. We have a God that walked the earth in the garden. We have a God that created the heaven and earth. We have a God that created us! We have a God that rules this universe.

We have a God that is love and created love. We have a God that loved us. We have a God that is our shepherd. We have a God that is our righteousness.

We have a God that makes the oceans claps and the seas praise him. All creation praises him. We have a God whose son is the bright and morning star. He is the lamb that was slain. He is the risen one. His King of King, He is Lord of Lords!

We have a God that that feels our pain. We have God who sent his son to know our pains and heal us. We have a God that never sleeps and never slumbers. We have a God that is always the same yesterday and tomorrow. We have a God that placed his gifts in us to glorify him. We have a God that gave us eternal life through Jesus. We have a God that created us to worship him.

Our God is holy! Our God is righteous is judgment. Our God is faithful. Our God is worthy of all praise. Our God is omnipotent. He is benevolence. He is patience. He is wise; He is perfect in all his ways. He is forever present. He is magnificent. He is mighty.

He is always available. He is the great prayer answered. He is a healer of the broken heart. He is a repairer of the wounded soul. He is a healer of the body and restores of the mind. He amazing and an awesome God. He is yours. He is mine! Who is this great creator? Our God... who is sovereign!

What did you get?

God gave us a prayer to talk, petition, give things, cry out, communion, worship, and communicate with him about our circumstance. In his sovereignty, He is God all by himself. He gives us through prayer the relationship restored by Jesus to ask of him what we need.

Prayer changes things

Pray with faith. Believe in God. Have faith in God and not in your ability to pray. In other words, keep your eyes on him. Keep your eyes on Jesus. We live by faith. When we pray, we are in the spirit. We are dealing with our problems on several fronts at one time, which is why your prayer feels full as you release yourself to the Holy Spirit. We are:

Approaching God with reverence
Recognizing his kingdom and his authority
Asking for God's for intervention
Speaking God's word back to him
Praying in son's name and power
Believing for results by faith
Attacking demons spirits with authority in Jesus name
Commanding evil to flee casting it out
Praying with power and expectation
Praising him for victory
Humbles before God throne for will to be done
Letting our faith rise up with hope
Thanking God for help
Listening for God to speak

Prayer is not a formula but a process of praying in the spirit to get results. Be led by the Holy Spirit. This framework is just an overview of different components of prayer you may experience as you pray for healing. We encourage people as they read our books to eventually put the books down and just pray as the Holy Spirit leads you.

Why are you sick?

There are many reasons why people get sick. There are some that believe that sickness comes from sin alone. However, there are times in the bible where Jesus healed for God to glorify and it did not sin. There are places in the bible where Jesus told people not to sin or they get sick again. Jesus cast out demons in the bible that caused sickness also.

Whether it is sin, diet, generational curse, witches, people that curse you, demons, culture, spells, accidents, childhood, birth defects, disasters, and spiritual attacks there is power in prayer to pray for healing. It is the prayer of faith that heals the sick. Prayer can be simple or it can be involved. But above all things ...pray!

"Rejoice always, pray without ceasing, and give thanks in all circumstances; for this is the will of God in Christ Jesus for you. Do not quench the Spirit. Do not despise prophecies, but test everything; hold fast what is good. Abstain from every form of evil. Now may the God of peace himself sanctify you completely, and may your whole spirit and soul and body be kept blameless at the coming of our Lord Jesus Christ. He who calls you is faithful; he will surely do it. Brothers, pray for us."
I Thessalonians 5: 16-25

Pray and believe

As you the prayer in this book may God ignite you in your faith. He is sovereign and he has compassion and answers prayer as he wills. We just pray, ask, and seek him for we need in healing and life. Healing is the mind, soul, and the spirit. Just ask him I prayer and believer. Jesus made a way for you to come to the father...so come n prayer believe that he is willing and able to answer your needs! Pray changes things! Your answer to your healing is just prayer away! Jesus is lord of all things. God will make a way! Have faith and believe! He is just a prayer away!

"And without faith, it is impossible to please Him, for he who comes to God must believe that He is and that He is a rewarder of those who seek Him. "Hebrews 11:6

"And He could do no miracle there except that He laid His hands on a few sick people and healed them. And He wondered at their unbelief. And He was going around the villages teaching. "Mark 6:5-6

"Therefore, confess your sins to one another, and pray for one another so that you may be healed. The effective prayer of a righteous man can accomplish much. Elijah was a man with a nature like ours, and he prayed earnestly that it would not rain, and it did not rain on the earth for three years and six months. Then he prayed again, and the sky poured rain and the earth produced its fruit. "James 5:16-18

We Always End
Our books with this...
Chapter 10

Prayer can change things! Over the years, I have read countless prayer books. I co-authored prayers in a book called "Prayers from the Heart" in 2000 with other Christian writers. The day the book was released nationally to bookstores all across the USA, my car caught on fire. My husband and I were astonished at the quick backlash that came from the publishing of a powerful prayer book. Over the last 20 years of walking with God, I have seen the power of prayer in action. I have also seen the warfare that follows from the enemy's attacks. Prayer moves God in the heaven on our behalf. Prayer is power. Prayer is a dangerous weapon in the wrong hands. Prayer is the key to a relationship with God, with Jesus, and with the world around us. We will always be faced with battles as long as we live in this world. The key is praying our way through and believing God for victory.

Jesus gave us the key to praying:

"And when you pray, you must not be like the hypocrites. For they love to stand and pray in the synagogues and at the street corners, that they may be seen by others.
Truly, I say to you, they have received their reward. But when you pray, go into your room and shut the door and pray to your Father who is in secret. And your Father who sees in secret will reward you. And when you pray, do not heap up empty phrases as the Gentiles do, for they think that they will be heard for their many words
Do not be like them, for your Father knows what you need before you ask him. Pray then like this: 'Our Father in heaven, hallowed be your name. Your kingdom comes, you will be done, on earth as it is in heaven. Give us this day our daily bread,
And forgive us our debts, as we also have forgiven our debtors.
And lead us not into temptation, but deliver us from evil.
For if you forgive others their trespasses, your heavenly Father will also forgive you, but if you do not forgive others their trespasses, neither will your Father forgive your trespasses. "Mathew 6:5-15

It would take whole books to really break down so many revelations and insights on this passage. This passage encourages the humility and sacredness of prayer along with the need to address heaven in prayer for our needs.

There are several types of prayers you will find in this passage:

Thanksgiving - Honoring God for who he is

Petition - Daily needs to be met

Praise - Hallowed be his name!

Intercession - Forgive others

Warfare - Deliver us from evil

Mercy - Forgive us, Lord

Deliverance - Deliverance from debt and evil

The power of prayer engaged with the Holy Spirit will ignite your prayer life. There is a war in the heavenlies and prayer is the key. It is important to pray always in the spirit when you pray and acknowledge God's power with faith in the midst of you.

Praying in the Spirit is not only praying in tongues, but it is also praying as led by the Spirit of God. Praying in the spirit means having the connection of faith, power, revelations, relationship, and discernment of the things of God. When you are baptized in the Holy Spirit, you have all you need to pray with power. I got baptized in the Holy Spirit in a hotel room seeking God's face. The power came over me and I began to weep.

For some, the Holy Spirit may move in many ways as he touches them. The Holy Spirit will always move with power whatever that may look like on an individual in a personal way. Expect God to move as you pray! Expect the Holy Spirit to guide you, lead you, and comfort you as you pray. Before we get started in prayer, you can pray at the end of this chapter to get refreshed with the Holy Spirit and allow God to use you in prayer for the issues in your life. We all have to fight in this life. But we need to fight with prayer using God's power in us! Jesus made a way for us to connect to God's power as we are walking with him! Pray and pray with the Power that Jesus provided!

Praying Prophetically
"To make known beforehand; to declare in advance"

Praying prophetically means praying in the Spirit in the gifting of God that he provided for what is to come. Prophecy means the fulfilling of God's word in our lives and others in a future tense. Praying prophetically is praying with the revelation of what is to come in the future and your prayers intercede for it to come to pass by the leading of the Holy Spirit. An excellent biblical example of this is John 17 when Jesus prayed for us before we even came into this world!

"For I have given them the words that you gave me, and they have received them and have come to know in truth that I came from you, and they have believed that you sent me.
I am praying for them. I am not praying for the world but for those whom you have given me, for they are yours.
All mine are yours, and yours are mine, and I am glorified in them.
And I am no longer in the world, but they are in the world, and I am coming to you. Holy Father, keep them in your name, which you have given me that they may be one, even as we are one."
John 17:8-11

Jesus prayed for the apostles, as they would go through many trials. But he also includes all those who would follow him through the work he did: namely believers in Christ Jesus. The gifts Jesus has, we have through accepting him. When we pray there is a beautiful combination of our gifting that comes through the way of the Holy Spirit that stirs up the atmosphere: faith, miracles, prophecy, word of wisdom, and word of knowledge to name a few.

There is no pattern to praying. There is the sincerity of heart and the openness to being used by God. Don't get this confused with psychic prayers, witchcraft, and false prophecy, which have flooded the airways of prayer. Always make sure you are walking in the Spirit of God, trying the spirits to make sure they are of God and discern God. I have heard prayers that were witchcraft, false prophetic, demonic, and evil-hearted. It is easy to slip into your flesh when you are not practicing the presence of God. By that, I mean experiencing God's presence on a regular basis where you can discern through the Holy Spirit what is of God. The key to that is prayer and more prayer. It is not how long you pray or if you pray out loud, or how 'spiritual' your prayer may be.

There is no length of time to praying. I asked God once about praying for hours and getting up early if that was something I should do. The Lord spoke to my heart that he was not concerned with me praying all morning but praying all day in relationship with him. In other words, just being sensitive to the Holy Spirit 24 hours a day to pray as needed. It is communing and dwelling with God in a personal way. It is allowing him to father you and be there 24 -7- 365! You can pray sitting quietly. You can pray with gospel music on. You can pray while taking a long walk. You can pray while cooking! You can commune with God anywhere through Christ Jesus! It is in your constant hunger for your relationship with God through Jesus Christ that causes prayer to be effective.

The prayers in this book are not expected to be a magic wand for your problems but an encouragement to prayer. I *do* believe that God will move and work in miracles! I am hoping as you pray you will *put* the book down and let God have his way! You will begin to pray with power and might as led by the Holy Spirit!
I hope that you will begin to break strongholds, draw close to God, and feel his presence in such a way that all you can do is weep in his presence!

This book is just a small stepping-stone to your victory to lead you to prayer in a closer way. There are no secret phrases or magic wands within these pages. Your family needs your prayers! The community needs your prayers! The lost need you! You are just as valuable and important as anyone else in the body of

Christ! God has called you to prayer. There is not an office in the Bible called 'intercessor', we are all to intercede one for another out of love through Christ Jesus. I have found most people who are 'intercessors' are actually prophets who have not been encouraged to walk out their office. The body of Christ at times has misused intercessors and they have the weight of the whole body of Christ on them. God is calling us all to pray and fellowship with him! It is meant to be the start of something great as you press into God with power, faith, and the blood of Jesus in prayer!

Take yourself in prayer daily to be cleansed and strengthened by God. Take your heart to God, your desires, and your soul! Your relationship with God through Jesus Christ is the key to prayer. He will lead you and guide you through his Holy Spirit as you open up to him. If you desire the gift of tongues then pray and He will answer your heart's desire. I have seen countless people filled with the gift of the Holy Spirit. The Holy Spirit is a gift that you can ask God for and receive as you open up your heart to hear and surrender to him. Be open to what God will do in Jesus' name! The prayer below is to be refreshed by the Holy Spirit and allow God to move. Let's get started and pray in Jesus' name!

"I will ask the Father, and he will give you another Helper, who will stay with you forever. He is the Spirit, who reveals the truth about God. The world cannot receive him because it cannot see him or know him. But you know him because he remains with you and is in you." John 14:16-17

"I will ask the Father, and he will give you another Helper, who will stay with you forever. He is the Spirit, who reveals the truth about God. The world cannot receive him because it cannot see him or know him. But you know him, because he remains with you and is in you." John 14:16-17

Prayer for the Holy Spirit

Lord, I come to you and ask that you baptize me and refresh me as needed now with your Holy Spirit. Forgive me for quenching the Holy Spirit in any way. Lord, I need your power, your Spirit, your word, and your will to be done in me. Fill me to overflowing, touch me, and refresh me now with your Holy Spirit. I open up my heart, my soul, and my mind, my whole being to you Jesus to come now and reside in me. Holy Spirit, guide in Jesus' name. Teach me to pray. Teach me about Jesus, teach me about the Father. Make me an open-ended vessel to your power Holy Spirit in Jesus' name. I receive your power now. I receive the gift of tongues if it is in your will. Heal me and strengthen me to walk with you, God. Help me to know your words and to pray as lead by you in all things. I surrender my life, my mind, and my ears to hear my heart to you now and receive your power now! I thank you, Jesus, for reviving your Holy Spirit in me this day. Keep me if I fall away and take full control of my life! I am renewed and refreshed this day by faith and I thank you Lord for touching me! In Jesus' name! I receive it by faith now!

Coffee with God
Prayer Changes Things!

Artist and Writer Bio Ramon & Janie McGee

"Over the years we have started many books but never had the time to finish them. In the last two years, we have been on a journey to self-publish our books. We have a lot to learn! However, we are writing books for the Black community to fill voids we found in the Christian book industry."

Ramon and Janie McGee are Writers with over 40 years experience. For the past 44 years, Janie McGee has created volumes of art telling the story of Black history in America. Her love for history began one summer on a project at the University of Cincinnati. She worked 10 weeks in the Harriet Beecher Stowe House creating mosaics depicting the Underground Railroad. That experience set a flame in her spirit to create images that tell the story of Blacks' struggles, and triumphs in America. Her studio Little Liza Jane produces fine art, décor, design, books, folk art, and art from the soul. Janie is a graduate of Ohio Dominican College from her native city of Columbus Ohio Ramon is a graduate from Princeton University. In the past 34 years, she has created a massive body of work that is on permanent display throughout the USA.

Janie started writing poetry and short stories at a very young age. She has been published on the web, in books, and in magazines. When she was in the military, she worked on special duty as a graphic artist and writer for the public affairs office. McGee wrote human-interest stories, interviews, and articles for the Army reserve. Over the years, she has co-authored a book of prayer with other writers called

"Prayers from the Heart" through Honor Books publishing. She also wrote Vacation Bible School (VBS) material and short stories for Cook Communications Ministries.

Ramon worked with the Christian retail marketing association many years ago. Janie was a special duty journalist for the military. Together their education, many years of ministry and desire for truth has put them us on a quest to write and produce art that reflects the word of God. Their desire to write books for the community with diversity is fueled by an urgency to heal and give hope. The racial atmosphere in America is getting worse. The Church is funding projects left and right. Meanwhile many are hurting. We don't expect our books to solve the problems in America. But we hope they provide creative solutions, heart, spirit, and hope.

Their family is very arty! They are always dancing, painting, writing, creating, and more! They have had several studios/galleries over the years. Because their family is on the move, they are providing the arts for purchase through their websites. You can purchase prints, books, and more. If you need more information, email them. They'd love to hear from you. Check out our blog also. They update their blogs regularly with articles and new happenings. Their business is Christian operated. Our products are created to inspire those who are seeking hope, truth, love, and art inspired by simple faith.

The McGee's have written for several small press newspapers across the USA. Their work reflects their love for humanity, God, and life. The McGee's love telling their stories through the combination of fine art, music, and writing. The McGee's has two children who are testimonies within themselves. Their son Jamile McGee and daughter Jasmine McGee are both gifted in the arts. Jamile was 3rd place winner of Fox TV's "So You Think You Can Dance?" Season 1. He has traveled the world dancing. Jamile was in Las Vegas on tour with

Wayne Brady. He is married to Angie McGee a new addition and blessing to their family. He teaches workshops and master classes along with his choreography. Jasmine is a college graduate, professional blogger, writer, and columnist for a Hip Hop magazine, a filmmaker, and an artist. She self-published her first book last year – Think Soul 25. Ramon edits and writes with Janie out of their home based studio Double Latte Books.

They have self-published 20 titles. She is working on several children's books for this year. You can find her artwork and prints at www.janiemcgee.com

"We want God to be exalted in all we do. I hope the art; books and material you come across in the future will draw you to Jesus and heal your life. May God get all of the Glory!"

Have Coffee with God and Pray!

Ramon & Janie McGee

Coffee with God
Prayer Changes Things!

Made in the USA
Columbia, SC
12 April 2019